David
Hockney

GREAT MOMENTS
IN PRO BASKETBALL

Colorful accounts of the men and teams responsible for 12 of pro basketball's greatest moments. Among other stories, the authors tell of the Washington Capitols' 17-game winning streak, Bob Cousy's quadruple overtime victory, the Globetrotters' defeat of the champion Minneapolis Lakers, Bob Pettit's revenge on the Celtics and Wilt Chamberlain's 100-point night.

Great Moments
in Pro Basketball

by DAVE WOLF and BILL BRUNS
Illustrated with Photographs

PRO
BASKETBALL
LIBRARY

Random House
New York

Photograph credits: Brown Brothers, 2, 13, 18; Harlem Globetrotters, 39, 42, 45; UPI, 9, 22, 30, 33, 49, 53, 71, 73, 76, 80, 82, 85, 106, 107, 110, 116, 122, 126, 143, 145, 149, 151, 154, 157 (bottom), 160, 162, 171; Wide World, 57, 63, 89, 101, 104, 115, 117, 121, 135, 136, 146, 157 (top), 165; John Zimmermann, *Life* Magazine ® Time, Inc., 170; cover photograph: *Sport* Magazine, Martin Blumenthal; front endpaper, Wide World; back endpaper, Ken Regan.

Text design by Jackie Mabli
Cover design by Ted Burwell

Library of Congress Catalog Card Number: 68-29584
Manufactured in the United States of America

CONTENTS

INTRODUCTION

In the last 70 years pro basketball has grown from a little-known sport, surviving on fans' contributions of nickels and dimes, to a multimillion dollar spectacle featuring the finest athletes in the world. In the process, there have been thousands of outstanding individual performances and hundreds of memorable games played by great pro clubs. In this book, we have tried to describe some of the best.

The Original Celtics, a swashbuckling troupe of basketball pioneers, were the first great pro team. In fact, they won so often and so convincingly that the American Basketball League had to take dramatic action to prevent them from destroying all competition.

The Washington Capitols came along almost 20 years later. Although they never won a league title, the Caps featured some of the game's top names: Red

Auerbach, Bones McKinney and Bob Feerick. Moreover, they focused attention on the still struggling sport by setting a record for consecutive victories that has never been surpassed.

In the years when the black man was barred from pro basketball's organized leagues, the Harlem Globetrotters—an all-Negro team—offered an opportunity to many talented players. The Globetrotters, who still entertain fans throughout the world, were more than exciting—they were also a solid team. And in 1948 and 1949 they proved their ability against the pro champions, the Minneapolis Lakers, and scored two of their most cherished victories.

Today, basketball is known for its high scorers. But in the late 1940s, when it was normal for a final score to read 70–65, Joe Fulks and George Mikan piled up totals that didin't become commonplace for another decade. Fulks was a lanky, 6-foot 5-inch jump shooter for the Philadelphia Warriors. In 1949 he set a scoring record that remained unbroken for 10 years.

The towering, 6-foot 10-inch Mikan did more than score for his team. He blocked shots, grabbed rebounds and helped establish the Minneapolis Lakers as the first championship dynasty in modern pro basketball. After winning six titles in seven years, the Lakers concluded their reign in a ferocious play-off series with Syracuse in 1954.

But the man who really put the National Basketball Association on the map was Bob Cousy of the Boston Celtics. For over a decade, the slick-passing guard thrilled fans with his brilliant ball handling, proving that the little man has a place in pro ball. We have selected what is probably his best performance, a quadruple-overtime game in the 1953 play-offs.

Cousy also played a major role in forming the next great dynasty. The Boston Celtics began their reign over pro basketball in 1957, when rookie Bill Russell, now recognized as the finest defensive center in history, arrived to pace them to a thrilling play-off victory over St. Louis. Although Boston won nine more championships in the next 11 years, this particular season was one of the team's finest.

Naturally, unseating a superclub like the Celtics required super players. And in 1958 Bob Pettit, a lean, 6-foot 9-inch forward, almost single-handedly carried St. Louis to the N.B.A. title with a tremendous scoring effort in the final game of the play-offs.

Nine seasons later, it was Wilt Chamberlain's turn. After years of frustration, the 7-foot 2-inch center finally played on a championship team when his Philadelphia 76ers defeated Boston. Wilt's new style, which emphasized passing, rebounding and defense, was a major factor in the 76ers' success.

Chamberlain appears in an earlier chapter, too. For in a book of "great moments," it would be impossible not to mention Wilt's record of 100 points in a single game—a mark that will probably never be broken.

Play-offs and All-Star games are usually filled with excitement. But few have surpassed the thrills of the 1954 All-Star game and the 1962 play-off finals. The latter stimulated amazing performances by a number of stars—Jerry West, Elgin Baylor, Bill Russell, Bob Cousy and Sam Jones—and the pulsating series went all the way to the seventh game.

The 1954 All-Star contest was more than a showcase of early N.B.A. heroes. It was a tension-packed struggle that reached its climax with one of the most dramatic moments in pro basketball.

Of course, there have been many other outstanding performances by such men as Oscar Robertson, Rick Barry, Willis Reed, Jerry Lucas and Paul Arizin. There have been other important team victories, too—for example, the Buffalo Germans' 111 straight wins between 1908 and 1911, the Rochester Royals' N.B.A. title victory in 1950 and the Celtics' dethroning of Chamberlain and the 76ers in 1968.

However, a book has a limited number of pages, so we have included only 12 stories. We hope we have successfully conveyed the sense of excitement and drama that ran through each of these great moments in pro basketball.

Dave Wolf and
Bill Bruns

one

THE FIRST SUPERCLUB

Players like Wilt Chamberlain, Bill Russell and Oscar Robertson today earn over $100,000 a year playing professional basketball. National Basketball Association games are viewed on television by millions of people. Teams roll up point totals in the hundreds, playing before packed houses from Madison Square Garden in New York to the Civic Auditorium in San Francisco. But pro basketball wasn't always like this.

The game of basketball was invented in 1891 by Dr. James Naismith, a gym instructor at Springfield College in Springfield, Massachusetts. Dr. Naismith visualized it as a mass-recreation activity employing an unlimited number of players on each side. Soon, however, the game became a popular competitive

Jim Furey, the Original Celtics' first owner, with Johnny Beckman.

sport and amateur teams began to spring up in the eastern United States. Professionalism followed quite naturally.

Whenever a pro team needed money to buy uniforms or rent a gymnasium, it passed a hat among the spectators, asking for contributions. If any money was left over after the debts had been paid, the players divided it. And if today's rules are used as a basis for judging professionalism, it can be said that Lambert Will, a star of the 1890s, gave up his amateur status for a mere 50 cents.

In the early years of the 20th Century, the leading teams boasted such exotic names as the Troy Trojans, the Oswego Indians, the Herkimer 31st Separate Company, the Buffalo Germans and the New York Whirlwinds. But it was not until the 1920s that a pro team commanded national interest and inspired fierce emotions in fans from coast to coast. This team was known as the Original Celtics, and it was the first superclub in the history of the game.

Until the Celtics came into prominence, pro basketball was a chaotic, disorganized sport. Players were not bound by contracts as they are today. And it was not unusual for fans to cheer their lungs out for a star, and then show up the following evening to find that he had switched uniforms and was playing for the opposing team.

Jim Furey, the Original Celtics' first owner, ended this practice. By 1921, most of the Celtics' stars had already joined the team, and that year Furey became the first owner to sign all his players to exclusive one-year contracts. If he hadn't, he might not have been able to hold the Celtics together very long. For every one of his players was in demand among the other pro teams. They were so good, in fact, that later the entire team was elected to the Basketball Hall of Fame.

The Celtics reached their peak in the "roaring twenties," which is also called the "Golden Age of Sport." It was an era of financial prosperity, when a large number of people had money in their pockets —and the desire to spend it watching sports events. The heroes of the time were such legendary figures as Babe Ruth, Jim Thorpe, Jack Dempsey, Red Grange and Bobby Jones. The Original Celtics, brilliant athletes and colorful personalities, fit perfectly into this brawling, exciting time.

In the early years, the Celtics' starting line-up included George "Horse" Haggerty as center, Nat Holman and fancy-shooting Johnny Beckman as guards, and Chris Leonard and Dutch Dehnert as forwards. Leonard was such a fine defensive player that his teammates called him "The Leech." Dehnert, despite his 5-foot 11-inch, 210-pound frame, had surprising speed and would often dazzle the fans with his tricky ball-handling.

Later, when Haggerty slowed down and Beckman was traded, the Celtics added center Joe Lapchick and forwards Davey Banks and Pete Barry. Banks had the best outside shot on the team and Barry was the first player to gain fame as a substitute. A hot-tempered, quick-fisted scrapper, he would often come off the bench to start a much-needed rally.

The Original Celtics' most colorful stars were Holman, Lapchick and Haggerty. Few players could pass the ball better than the handsome, 5-foot 11-inch, 175-pound Holman. Blessed with superb poise —which was sometimes mistaken for arrogance— Nat was also the team leader and one of its top scorers. He later became a famous coach at City College of New York.

In those days, the slender, 6-foot 5-inch Lapchick was considered a "giant." But, in spite of his size, Joe had excellent coordination. At a time when most big men had trouble running from one end of the court to the other without falling down, Lapchick was a good leaper and a fine shot. He was the first of the running and jumping centers, who now dominate basketball. After his playing career ended, Joe coached the New York Knickerbockers in the N.B.A. and championship teams at St. Johns University.

Haggerty preceded Lapchick at center for the Celtics. Nicknamed "The Horse," Haggerty wasn't very fast and didn't do much scoring, but he made his 6-foot 4-inch, 235-pound body felt around the boards. He was a muscular man, who reminded many fans of the fabled woodsman, Paul Bunyan. One of Haggerty's jobs was to protect his smaller teammates if the opposition tried to get rough.

The Celtics played a brand of basketball that was a far cry from today's fast-paced, high-scoring game. The courts of the 1920s were much shorter and most were enclosed by a net made of cord or wire. As a result, the ball could never go out of bounds, for if it hit the net it was still in play. Fans used to joke that basketball was played in a cage—and this is how the players came to be known as "cagers."

Each half was 20 minutes long, but unlike today the clock continued to run during free throws and jump balls. It stopped only during time-outs and the frequent fights. After each basket the teams returned to midcourt for a jump ball. This last rule was very helpful to the Celtics. Since Haggerty and, later, Lapchick were tall enough to control almost every tap, their opponents sometimes played 10 minutes without *touching* the ball.

However, game scores were usually low. The

Nat Holman

Celtics, who often made 40 points in a game, were held in awe. Along with the fact that the shooters of the 1920s were not as tall or as skilled as today's stars, there were several other reasons for the low scoring games. First, the "running clock" and the jump balls after each basket left little actual playing time. Second, the baskets did not present a very easy target. Most extended so far from the backboards that carom shots were almost impossible. Even lay-ups were difficult. Usually, it was "swish" or nothing. Sometimes there were no backboards at all—just a basket hung at the end of a long metal pole supported by ropes running into the stands.

Basketball was a raw, rough game and not for the weak of heart. "To stay in one piece," recalls Holman, "you had to wear hip pads, elbow pads, aluminum cups and knee guards. Even then you weren't safe. The audience would often drop lighted cigarets from overhanging balconies or reach through the net to trip you as you came running down court."

In this climate of rough-and-tumble basketball, the first great Celtic team took to the road in October, 1921. They won the championship in the Eastern Professional League, one of many local leagues existing at that time. But they spent most of the winter barnstorming through the Midwest and the South, popularizing the game wherever they went.

The Celtics lived a carefree, vagabond life—playing in dance halls, armories, auditoriums and large, smoke-filled rooms. They were tough, hard-drinking, fun-loving guys who rarely bothered with training rules. Even their owners were unusual. Jim Furey, the first owner, had to give up the team when he was sent to Sing Sing prison for embezzlement. His successor was a mysterious little fellow named Donovan, whom the players met only once. Donovan explained that the pressure of his "outside business" prevented him from spending much time with them. Soon afterward, Donovan was shot down by rival "business associates" in a hail of machine-gun bullets. This was the Prohibition era, when the sale of liquor was illegal, and Mr. Donovan's "outside business" turned out to be gangland rum-running.

The Celtics found a new owner, however, and continued to blaze a trail of victories across the country. "Our success was not accidental," Lapchick has said. "We were always talking basketball and experimenting with new plays. I believe we were twenty years ahead of our time. The Celtics introduced switching on defense, the give-and-go play and the pivot play."

The Celtics were proudest of their defense. They guarded their opponents so closely that their motto was: "Don't let your man breathe." On offense they used a deliberate style that emphasized sharp passing and ball handling. They worked patiently for a good shot and scored only on lay-ups and set shots. No one even considered the fast break or the jump shot, which are basic ingredients in today's run-and-shoot style. "You never dared take a shot unless you could be ninety-percent certain of making it," Lapchick once recalled.

"The Celtics took only perfect shots. We made well over fifty percent."

Most important to the Original Celtics was their fierce team pride. "We wouldn't tolerate mistakes, let alone defeats," Lapchick went on. "And that's why we continued to win, year after year. We had tremendous pride in ourselves and in our team. When we lost a game the dressing room was an awful place. Tempers were vicious and recriminations sometimes were physical."

But the Celtics rarely lost. Playing almost exclusively on the road, before hostile fans and partisan referees, they won well over 90 percent of their games. Fans either loved the Original Celtics for their great ability or hated them for their confident style. The loudest boos were reserved for Holman because he was the top player in the game and didn't let the fans forget it. Once, when Holman stepped up to the foul line in a Midwest town, the local fans tried, as usual, to disconcert him by screaming and booing. To show his disdain, the cocky forward stared coldly at the crowd without even glancing at the basket. Then, with his eyes still fixed on the fans, he flipped the ball through the hoop. "I was lucky that the ball dropped in," he later said with a smile. "Otherwise I could never have lived it down."

The greatness of the Celtics was most clearly

shown by their ability to win on the road, where most visiting teams never had a chance. In those days, hometown clubs rarely lost because they had the referee and the crowd on their side. In tough Pennsylvania mining towns, where the betting was usually heavy, it was a common practice for fans to shake the supports of the baskets as a visiting player prepared to take a free throw.

Chris Leonard

An example of such hometown "spirit" occurred one night when the Celtics were playing in Carbondale, Pennsylvania, before 2,000 angry-looking miners. With the score tied, 28-28, in the closing seconds, the star of the home team grabbed the basket with one hand and pulled himself up like a monkey. Hanging from the rim, he took a pass with his free hand and dropped in the winning shot. The Celtics protested vigorously, but the referee needed only one look at the 2,000 grisly, bearded miners to make up his mind. As far as he was concerned, the basket was good and the local team had won.

But this sort of thing didn't happen to the Celtics very often. Usually they were so good that even a dishonest referee couldn't keep them from winning. To make sure, however, they developed a few methods for dealing with unfair officials.

For example, during a time-out one evening, they noticed the referee talking earnestly to their rivals. Dutch Dehnert was suspicious. Quietly he slipped over to listen in on the conversation. "Take it easy, boys," he overheard the official say. "I'll call so many fouls on the Celtics you'll win without any trouble."

When Dehnert relayed these words to the other Celtics, they decided to take quick action. As the referee tossed up a jump ball at midcourt, Johnny

Beckman hit him high and Dehnert hit him low. The man crumpled in a heap on the floor. Then Haggerty rushed to the sidelines, grabbed a bucket of water and gleefully dumped the entire pail on the unconscious referee.

"Where am I?" gasped the official, trying to shake the cobwebs from his brain.

"You're practically in the trash can," growled the huge Haggerty. "Call them honestly or we'll really go to work on you!"

Needless to say, the referee called the game honestly from then on. And, of course, the Celtics won.

In 1925 the Celtics were offered a chance to join the newly formed American Basketball League. There had been many leagues in the past, but the A.B.L. was the first attempt to organize one that was national in scope. It was a good idea, but the Original Celtics wanted no part of the A.B.L. For them, barnstorming through the country was much more profitable. They played exhibition games against league teams, however, and always routed them.

In the league's first year, Cleveland won the championship. But it was a hollow triumph, for the Celtics were still considered the best team in pro basketball. In the 1926-27 season they actually became a threat to the league's survival. As they continued to beat league members, the A.B.L. lost its credibility and attendance began to fall off. Then the A.B.L. owners made a smart move. They decided that no league team would play the Celtics. This sharply cut the Celtics' profits and soon the prodigal sons asked to join the A.B.L.

As a "reward" for their crimes, the Celtics were given the defunct Brooklyn franchise, which was already in last place. At the time, the season was divided in halves, and the Celtics were too far behind to win the opening section. But they made a shambles of the second-half race, finishing first with a record of 19 wins and one loss. Then they met Cleveland in a series to settle the first real national pro championship. And the Original Celtics won easily, 29-21, 28-20 and 35-32.

For the 1927-28 season, the American Basketball League was divided into Eastern and Western divisions. But the Celtics kept on rolling up victories. Representing New York this time, they won the Eastern title with a record of 40 wins and nine losses. Then they moved into the five-game "World Series" against the Fort Wayne Hoosiers.

The first three games were scheduled for Fort Wayne. In spite of the Hoosiers' home-court advantage, the Celtics burst quickly ahead in the opener. Lapchick dominated his opponent in the crucial jump balls after each basket. Holman and

Banks hit with two-handed set shots from outside. The Celtics' defense never let the Hoosiers get organized. By half time the Celtics were in command, 14-6.

In the last half, Fort Wayne played their opponents on even terms. But for every basket by the Indiana team, Holman, Barry or Lapchick would come back quickly to score. The Celtics won, 30-21.

The Celtics began the second game as though it was going to be another easy victory and by half time led, 15-8. But the Hoosiers were also a proud team and were fired up for the last half. Suddenly the Celtics were in trouble. As the crowd of over 4,000 applauded wildly, Fort Wayne broke through the Celtics' vaunted defense to chop away at the lead. The Hoosiers increased the speed of their attack even more, snapping fast passes and tossing in quick shots.

With 8 minutes remaining in the game, Frank Shimek drove in for a lay-up and Fort Wayne tied the score, 19-19. The Celtics were unable to penetrate the Hoosiers' aroused defense and had to resort to outside shooting. But their shots were off target.

Fort Wayne held Holman to just two points and Lapchick to four, and went on to even the series with a startling 28-21 victory. The Celtics had

Pete Barry

scored only six points in the last half.

Their reputation—and their title—was in danger. But in the third game they came charging back and moved to a 15-10 first-half lead. In the last half Lapchick moved smoothly around the basket, grabbing rebounds and drawing fouls, and Banks swished set shots over the Hoosiers' defense. The Celtics won, 35-18, and headed home happy and confident of victory in the fourth game.

A crowd of over 3,000 jammed Arcadia Hall in Brooklyn. The Celtics' offense was superb. Holman, Barry and Banks whipped passes through the Fort

Wayne defense, continually springing a man open for an easy lay-up shot. With Lapchick dominating the backboards and controlling the center taps, Fort Wayne rarely had the ball. In the first half the Hoosiers could manage only one field goal and the Celtics galloped to a 16-4 lead.

But once again, Fort Wayne was a different team in the last half. Within a few minutes they scored 10 straight points. The crowd was stunned. The Celtics led by only a slim 16-14 margin.

They called a time-out. In the huddle the Celtics reminded each other that they could not afford another defeat. If the series went as far as the fifth game, anything could happen. They had to wrap it up now.

After the game resumed they carefully maneuvered Barry clear for a long set-shot. The crowd cheered wildly as the ball swished through the hoop. Then Ralph Miller of Fort Wayne cut the margin again to two points. But the Celtics suddenly broke loose, pouring in nine points to increase their lead to 27-18.

The Hoosiers fought back doggedly and the Celtics' lead began to dwindle again. The fans were standing, imploring them to hold on. A foul shot by Miller cut the score to 27-26. Less than a minute remained. The Celtics were under terrific pressure and now was the time to prove their greatness.

Lapchick thrust himself into the air, straining to control the tap. His fingers hit the ball and slapped it to Holman. Time was running out. Holman whipped the ball to Dehnert, who fired a quick pass to Banks. Holman took the pass from Banks and began to dribble. The frantic Hoosiers couldn't take the ball away and the game ended with the Celtics ahead, 27-26. They were the champions of the A.B.L. for the second year in a row.

Ironically, this triumph marked the end of their reign. They had become so superior to the rest of the league that they threatened to destroy all competition. Fans were turning out only to watch the Celtics. So, in perhaps the greatest tribute ever paid to a pro team, A.B.L. officials decided to break up the Celtics and distribute the players among the other teams in the league.

Years later, some of the original team joined under the Celtic banner to form a barnstorming team. But it was not the same, for the sport was changing. Soon the "cages" were removed from the sides of the court; the center jump after each basket was eliminated; and players began shooting more jump shots.

But the Original Celtics will never be forgotten. Their brilliant, imaginative play spread the game throughout the country. They were the best of their era—pro basketball's first superclub.

two

17 STRAIGHT FOR WASHINGTON

The American Basketball League continued to operate for decades after the breakup of the Original Celtics. But up to the end of World War II, sports fans still didn't regard pro basketball as a big league sport. And though college basketball was very popular, few big-city promoters wanted anything to do with the pros. Many of the pro teams were honest, but too many others were fly-by-night groups that toured the country playing one-night stands. Some teams thought little of cheating their opponents out of a share of the gate or playing rough, dirty ball.

During the war, however, so many servicemen played basketball that when peace came many leading arena owners decided the pro sport should move into the "big time." As a result, the National Basketball League was formed in 1945. A year later the Basketball Association of America was created, and this eventually became the National Basketball Association.

The Washington, D.C. franchise of the B.A.A. was headed by Mike Uline, who owned the Uline Arena. Uline knew nothing about basketball. But fortunately for him—and for the sport—he received a visitor shortly after he announced his decision to run the club. The visitor was Arnold "Red" Auerbach. Years later, as coach of the Boston Celtics, Auerbach would be regarded as the reigning genius of pro basketball. But at the time Red was a brash 28-year-old just out of the Navy and looking for a job.

Auerbach, who had been a smart, but far from great, player at George Washington University, had run a recreation program while in the service and had a master's degree in physical education. These credentials would hardly qualify him for an N.B.A. coaching job today, but Uline was desperate for anyone who could help him field a team. So Auerbach became the coach of the Washington Capitols.

Red was better prepared for the job than Uline had dared hope. While in the Navy, Auerbach had collected the addresses of many top basketball

Red Auerbach as coach of the Was⋅⋅ ⋅gton Capitols.

players. Now he knew where to reach them. Just as important, Red had played college ball for Bill Reinhardt, a coach whose thinking had been years ahead of his time. In those days, each section of the country had a very distinct style of basketball and most coaches preferred to use only players from their areas.

"The kids from New York were good at ball handling, the two-handed set shot and using a picture defense," Auerbach has recalled. "The Midwest was noted for its fast-break running and the West Coast specialized in jumping, rebounding and the one-handed shot. Reinhardt was the first coach to mold those styles together on one team."

Red set out to do the same thing in the pros. From the Midwest he signed 6-foot 3-inch John Norlander of Hamline University, a swift forward. From the East he took two excellent ball handlers, 6-foot 2-inch Irv Torgoff of Long Island University and 6-foot 8-inch John Mahnken of Georgetown University, one of the tallest centers in the league.

Red obtained much of his shooting strength from the West Coast. Fred Scolari (5 feet 10 inches) from the University of San Francisco went on to average 12.6 in the 1946 season, while Bob Feerick (6 feet 3 inches) from the University of Santa Clara led the Caps with a 16.8 average, second best in the B.A.A.

After joining the team, Feerick told Auerbach about Horace "Bones" McKinney, a lean, colorful, 6-foot 6-inch forward from the University of North Carolina. McKinney, who later became a Baptist minister and the head coach at Wake Forest University, had already agreed to sign with the Chicago Stags. He even had a train ticket for Chicago. But since his train stopped in Washington, he told Feerick, an old friend from the Army, that he would at least talk to Red. And that was all the persuasive Auerbach needed. McKinney never got back on the train. Before the irate Chicago team knew what had happened, McKinney had signed his contract in the rest room of a Washington restaurant. He went on to become the Capitols' most popular player, averaging 12 points a game.

From the beginning of his coaching career Auerbach was a hard-driving taskmaster. He drilled his team in fundamentals and taught them how to work as a unit. When the season started he felt the Capitols had a chance to win the Eastern division title.

The Caps opened the 1946-47 season on the road with victories over Detroit and Pittsburgh. But just when Auerbach was starting to enjoy things, the high-scoring Feerick injured his ankle at St. Louis. The Caps lost that game, 70-69, and went on to be routed at Cleveland, 92-68. With Feerick still out of the line-up, they traveled to Philadelphia to meet the unbeaten Warriors.

When the game began, Auerbach couldn't believe his eyes. Washington missed its first 19 shots from the floor and trailed, 16-2, before hitting a field goal. With 10 minutes left in the game, the Warriors increased their lead to 61-42 and many fans began leaving. But suddenly McKinney caught fire and the rest of the team ignited with him. Bones hit shot after shot as the Caps rolled up 16 straight points. Though Philadelphia held on to win, 68-65, McKinney finished with 26 points and Washington gave the B.A.A. a glimpse into the future.

On November 16 the Caps met the Stags at Chicago Stadium. Washington was tied for fourth place in the six-team Eastern division with a record of two wins and three losses. In contrast, the Stags were leading the West and had won five of their six games. But even though Feerick was still out of the line-up, the Capitols upset Chicago, 73-65. It was the start of a winning streak that has yet to be surpassed.

On November 20 the St. Louis Bombers helped the Caps inaugurate big-league basketball in Washington. Unfortunately, they had to do it in something less than big-league style. The teams arrived at Uline Arena to find the backboards swaying crazily from guide wires. Even worse, the floor had been put down over a hockey rink and the ice had created slippery spots all over the court.

The game was closer to comedy than it was to basketball. Players who dared to drive invariably went skidding across the baseline like clowns in the circus. Finally, they resorted to long range shooting at the swinging targets.

Nevertheless, conditions were equal for both teams and the Caps had no intention of losing their home opener—even if only 2,500 fans had come out to welcome them. With three minutes remaining, St. Louis led, 50-49. Then Irv Torgoff, who hadn't scored a point all night, hit a foul shot to tie the score and, a moment later, sent Washington ahead by stealing the ball and sinking a lay-up. When St. Louis lost the ball again, the Caps stalled out the final seconds until Mahnken was fouled. He sank both shots and Washington went on to win, 54-51.

The Bombers' coach, Ken Loeffler, was furious. After the game he burst into the office of the Capitols' publicity manager, Paul Rothgeb, and shouted, "I won't bring my team to Washington again unless you give me a written guarantee that the conditions on this court have been remedied!"

Loeffler had a good argument, but that didn't dampen the Caps' thrill over winning their first home game. In fact, even after the baskets and floor were fixed, they won an incredible 29 of 30 games at Uline that season.

The next evening the Providence Steamrollers came to town and gave the Caps a scare. With guard George Mearns hitting from the outside, Providence led, 50-43, going into the fourth quarter. Fortunately, Feerick had returned to the lineup. He and Torgoff started scoring and McKinney and Mahnken took control of the boards. Auerbach's club scored 23 points in the last 12 minutes and went on to win, 66-58. The victory left them in second place, half a game behind the New York Knickerbockers.

Two nights later the Caps increased their winning

streak to four games by routing the Toronto Huskies at Uline Arena, 74-50. It was a rough game and 48 fouls were called. But Feerick maneuvered through a hail of elbows to score 20 points. Norlander scored 15 and Washington's fast break left the Huskies gasping for breath. The teams met again in Toronto on November 26th and the result was the same. This time the score was 73-68.

Soon it began to dawn on the players that an unusually long winning streak was developing. And to preserve it the superstitious McKinney started to take some strange precautions. Each day, for good luck, he repeated everything he had done on the day of the first victory. Bones insisted on eating the same food, wearing the same clothes and occupying the same spot on the bench. He even demanded that his teammates file in and out of the dressing room in the same order. "I used to drive my wife nuts rinsing those same orange-colored socks I wore every day," he said later. "And I made her make the same kind of soft scrambled eggs every morning for breakfast."

Whenever the team was at home, the players knew that at 2 o'clock in the afternoon they could be sure to find Bones at a certain used-car lot. But he wasn't shopping for a car. He was just making sure to visit the same places and talk to the same people at the same time he had the day Washington opened its home season against St. Louis.

Although McKinney's superstitious behavior may not have helped, the Caps continued to win. On November 27 Feerick scored 21 points to spark a 75-67 victory over Chicago. Then Washington beat Pittsburgh, 49-40, and Providence, 80-62, to increase its streak to eight. But on December 4, the Knicks won their ninth straight and still clung to a one-game lead. The following night, however, Philadelphia upset the Knicks, 62-51, and Washington moved within a half game of first place.

Two days later, against Detroit, the Caps won their ninth in a row and McKinney "invented" an unusual play. In the second quarter, one of the Falcons pushed him so far out of bounds that Bones crashed into the first row of temporary seats behind the basket. Chairs flew all over the court. Detroit hurriedly moved the ball toward the other basket, but Bones nonchalantly got up and began to remove the chairs from the playing surface. Washington fans screamed at McKinney to get back on defense, but Bones just grinned and continued his housekeeping until Scolari suddenly stole the ball. And, of course, McKinney was all alone under the opposite basket. The Falcons watched helplessly and the crowd roared with laughter as Scolari tossed a long pass to Bones, who dropped in an easy lay-up. Washington won,

"Bones" McKinney drives past Gale Bishop (11) of the Philadelphia Warriors.

75-64, and two days later repeated its victory over Detroit by a score of 81-66.

The Knicks were winning again, however, and the Capitols' record of 12 wins and three losses put them a game behind New York. Their next game was in Philadelphia, where they had to contend not only with the Warriors, but with a wet, slippery floor, much like the one at Uline on opening night. But the Caps were too hot to let anything bother them—even the hostile yelling of over 7,000 fans.

They jumped ahead, 32-20, at the half. Although Philadelphia closed the gap to 39-37 with 10 minutes left, Washington quickly broke the game wide open when Norlander, Scolari and McKinney (who shouted "swish" each time he shot) hit again and again. It was a clear-cut 64-49 victory—the Caps' 11th straight.

By now McKinney had a small, bare-bellied oriental doll, which had been sent to him by a fan. Bones named it "Yehudi" and added it to his superstitions. Before each game he demanded that every Capitol kiss "Yehudi" on the stomach before taking the court.

Back in Washington the Caps routed the Cleveland Rebels, the only club to beat them decisively. Little Scolari, who scored 16 points, controlled the game with his quick dribbling and passing and bombed the Rebels' defense with long one-handers.

Washington won even more easily than the 72-52 score indicated.

Now the Caps were really rolling. Their defense, led by McKinney, was the toughest in the league. And their superb passing allowed them to work men clear for open shots. On December 15, they finally moved into undisputed possession of first place—without playing. The Knicks, who had fallen into a slump, were crushed by Cleveland, 70-52, giving Washington a half-game lead.

But the St. Louis Bombers were still disdainful of the Caps' record and when they returned to Uline, Coach Loeffler boasted that if the baskets had stopped swinging and the floor was dry, his team would win. The fired-up Washington club responded by stepping into an early lead, prompting the frustrated Bombers to turn the game into the roughest of the season. Two St. Louis players fouled out and another was ejected from the game for shoving Norlander. Then, with five minutes left and the Caps ahead by 16 points, the Bombers' Aubrey Davis collided with Feerick, who reinjured his ankle and had to leave the game. Even without Feerick, the Caps went on to prove Coach Loeffler wrong by a lopsided score of 68-47.

With Feerick out of the line-up, it seemed that the Caps were in for trouble in their upcoming game with Philadelphia. The last time he'd been injured they had lost three straight. But nothing could stop them now. At half time, Washington led, 39-19. The margin was 56-32 when Auerbach began to send in his substitutes, and the Capitols coasted home, 68-56.

The day after Christmas, the Caps won their 15th game in a row at Providence, 78-66, and moved three-and-a-half games ahead of the sagging Knicks. "We have a fine streak," warned the delighted yet wary Auerbach, "but we can't underestimate anyone. New York can still give us a lot of trouble."

Three nights later the Caps had their showdown with the Knicks. Everyone had expected a tough game and, as a result, McKinney had taken extra pains to reach the used-car lot at exactly 2 o'clock. But the Caps turned the contest into a rout and won by a score of 70-49. In the fourth quarter, Norlander's third straight field goal gave them a 67-33 lead and Auerbach's substitutes had to resort to trick shots and fancy passes to keep the score down. It was Washington's 16th victory in a row.

The following night at Boston, the Caps showed signs of finally beginning to tire. And some observers thought they were getting a little overconfident, too. The last-place Celtics nearly accomplished the upset of the season when Connie Simmons tied the game, 57-57, with a last-second

McKinney scores against the Knicks.

hook shot. Consequently, the teams went into overtime. On the bench, Auerbach was in a rage. His team got the message. McKinney and Norlander started to hit the basket. The Caps' defense held Boston to three points in the overtime and Washington won its 17th straight by a score of 70-60.

Then on January 1, 1947, McKinney's lucky doll, "Yehudi," failed him at last. The Falcons, who had lost seven straight, almost blew Washington off the court in Detroit. The score was 35-17 at half time. The Capitols were stunned. Going into the fourth quarter they trailed, 54-36. Then they made a final valiant charge. But it was too late. Detroit won, 62-57. McKinney tossed "Yehudi" into the crowd. The 17-game streak had been broken.

Washington didn't let the loss bother them for long, however. The Caps went on to win the regular season title with an amazing total of 49 wins and 11 loses. But what their fans still remember is the record of 17 successive wins.

Basketball has come a long way since 1946 and the Washington Capitols have long been out of existence. But no team has broken the Caps' mark. The only club to tie the record was the Boston Celtics of 1959-60—and they too were coached by a man named Red Auerbach.

three

MORE THAN JUST CLOWNS

Pro basketball today is dominated by the black athlete. Of the ten players on the 1968 All-N.B.A. team, seven were black, including Wilt Chamberlain, Oscar Robertson, Elgin Baylor, Dave Bing, Bill Russell, Willis Reed and Hal Greer. That year, all the starters on the defending-champion Philadelphia 76'ers were black. But it was not always that way. Not until Chuck Cooper joined the Boston Celtics in 1950 was the color barrier broken in the N.B.A. Before that, black players usually had to retire after college or play in obscurity with barnstorming black teams. They had but one hope to achieve fame and an adequate income—to play with the Harlem Globetrotters. For the 'Trotters were world-famous. During the 1930s and 1940s they were basketball's most colorful and successful team—white or black.

The Globetrotters were organized in 1927 by a fearless little (5-foot 5-inches tall) promoter named Abe Saperstein. When he first took his team on the road in a battered Model-T automobile, Abe had just five players. He had to act as owner, coach, driver, trainer, substitute and water boy. The team was so poor in the early years that they often slept in town jails because they couldn't afford a hotel. Once, stranded by a blizzard in Montana, they had to spend three days in a tiny shack with a sheep-herder and his nine sheep. Often they would eat only hamburgers for days on end until they could afford a full meal.

Despite these initial hardships the Globetrotters survived to become basketball's biggest attraction. They played seven nights a week for six months of the year, packing arenas from New York City to Moose Jaw, Saskatchewan. Once they drew 35,000 for a game in the Pasadena Rose Bowl.

Like the Original Celtics, the 'Trotters were bas-ketball wizards. They could shoot, pass and handle the ball with dazzling skill. What made them famous, though, was their ability to make people laugh. They were the funniest team ever to play the game. The fans would double over in laughter when the 'Trotters began toying with their opponents: throwing behind-the-back passes that seldom missed, spinning the ball off their index fingers, bouncing the ball off their heads into the basket, or throwing passes between the legs of defenders. Most of the 'Trotters had such powerful hands that they could handle the ball as if it was an orange, befuddling the opposition with fancy ball-handling tricks.

Unfortunately, few people took their basketball skills seriously. They felt the 'Trotters were more interested in laughs than baskets. The astute Saperstein recognized this dilemma early in the team's career. "No matter how funny we are," he warned his players, "we've got to show people how well we play, too. Some day we're going to be accused of being just clowns. That's when we'll have to show that we can play as well as anyone."

His fears were realized the day of a game with a Canadian All-Star team, when a local sports reporter wrote: "All the Globetrotters can do is clown. If they had to play straight basketball anybody could beat them."

So the 'Trotters decided to play straight basketball with no laughs. The final score was: Globetrotters 122, Canadians 20.

Despite such examples of their ability, most people continued to feel that teams from the established pro leagues, the B.A.A. and the N.B.L., would run the 'Trotters off the court. How could they possibly contain George Mikan and the Minneapolis Lakers? Mikan, who stood 6-feet 10-inches tall, was the greatest scorer and rebounder in the history of the game. The Lakers were regarded as the best team in the country and were on their way to the 1947-48 N.B.L. title. But the Globetrotters' supporters stood firm. They claimed *their* team was the best— period! The arguments flew back and forth. Finally the two teams agreed to meet in Chicago to decide, once and for all, who was best.

The showdown was arranged for February 19, 1948, and was rightfully billed as "The Pro Basketball Game of the Year." A crowd of 17,853—the largest ever to see a pro game in Chicago—jammed into the Stadium. Because the local pro team, the Stags, was in the rival B.A.A. most of the spectators came to cheer the underdog 'Trotters.

There was also considerable speculation about the duel between Mikan and Globetrotter center Reece "Goose" Tatum. Goose was only 6 feet 3 inches tall, but he had exceptionally long arms and large hands that dangled down around his knees. His goal in life was "to make people laugh." It wasn't hard because he had an uninhibited flair for showmanship—playing tricks with the ball and leading the team's comic routines.

However, after the game started it soon became

Louis Pressley (left) and Ermer Robinson (right) haven't been able to prevent Mikan from sinking his shot.

obvious that Tatum and the Globetrotters wouldn't have many laughs that night. They were nearly exhausted from having played five games in five nights. And their playing showed the strain. Mikan and his rugged teammate, 6-foot 5-inch forward Jim Pollard, were dominating the boards. The huge, aggressive Mikan was simply overpowering Tatum. Yet Goose managed to deflect passes so often with his long arms that Mikan seldom had the ball to shoot. Nevertheless, Mikan scored 11 points and Pollard added 10 to put the Lakers ahead at half time, 32-23.

Even 'Trotter supporters saw little hope in the last half. There seemed no way to stop Mikan and Pollard. The Lakers' big men appeared to be enjoying a private game of volleyball, tapping the ball back and forth on the offensive backboards.

Finally the 'Trotters gambled, using two and even three men to guard Mikan, often fouling him. Although "Big George" kept scoring, he got the ball even less often than before and missed many of his foul shots. With the pressure now on their shoulders, the other Lakers began to wilt.

Ermer Robinson, the Globetrotters' slender 6-foot 3-inch forward, and Marques Haynes, famous for his brilliant dribbling acts, began to pop in long set-shots. Suddenly it was a new ball game.

Haynes' flashy passes and gaudy dribbling opened up the Lakers' defense and Tatum and Robinson slipped inside for easy baskets. Now the 'Trotters were in high gear and their rooters were going wild. The flustered Lakers began rushing their shots and losing the ball with bad passes. Gradually the 'Trotters closed the gap. Then Robinson sank a long shot from the corner to tie the game, 42-42. But there was still a quarter left to play.

Mikan and Pollard began to pour in points again (finishing with 24 and 18 points respectively), but the 'Trotters refused to fold. Six times the lead changed hands, and the play got rougher. Obviously, neither team was playing for laughs. Only once did the 'Trotters try any of their tricks. Robinson rolled the ball between a Laker's legs to Tatum, who snatched it up, whirled and dunked it. The crowd applauded, but the 'Trotters knew they couldn't afford to gamble with their clowning very often.

An outside set-shot by Haynes put the Trotters ahead, 59-58, with just under two minutes left to play. Then the Lakers moved downcourt and fed the ball to Mikan, who drove for the basket and was fouled by Tatum. Mikan had already missed seven free throws, but he calmly sank the penalty shot to tie the score, 59-59. Just one minute and 30 seconds remained.

Now the crowd was on their feet. They screamed encouragement as the 'Trotters began weaving nearer and nearer the basket, searching for one last shot. But the Laker defense wouldn't yield an opening. So the 'Trotters passed the ball around as if it were on a string. Then, just as time was running out, Robinson worked himself free 20 feet from the basket. Haynes spotted him and fired a quick pass. Robinson set loose his favorite two-

Robinson shoots over Mikan's outstretched hand.

handed shot. It arched toward the basket as the buzzer went off. Swish!—the 'Trotters had won, 61-59. The crowd stormed onto the court and the jubilant 'Trotters carried Saperstein and Robinson off on their shoulders. They had worked 20 years for this victory and they were going to savor every moment.

But a rematch was already brewing. The Lakers were embarrassed and incensed. They vigorously protested that Robinson's final shot had left his hands after the gun sounded. One timer agreed with them, but the other claimed that Robinson's shot had been good. The official ruling supported the 'Trotters, yet it was obvious that a rematch was needed.

It wasn't hard to arrange another game. The 'Trotters were confident of winning again and besides, they would be paid a good deal of money for playing. On their part, the Lakers needed to regain their injured pride and reputation. So a year later the two teams met again in Chicago. This time there was a crowd of 20,046 and over 5,000 people were turned away at the gate.

The Lakers were now in the B.A.A. and on their way to another championship. Mikan, again the league's leading scorer with nearly a 30-point average, was fresh from a 53-point effort against Baltimore two days earlier. But this year he would have a tougher match at center. The 'Trotters had Nat "Sweetwater" Clifton, an exciting 6-foot 7-inch rookie. Clifton, who was just out of high school, later starred with the New York Knicks in the N.B.A.

Once more the Globetrotters had trouble finding the range early in the game. They trailed, 8-1, after five minutes, 13-9 at the quarter and 24-18 at the half. The usually dead-eyed 'Trotters had missed nine of 11 free throws. Only the absence of the

Lakers' starting forwards, Pollard and Don Carlson, plus the fact that Clifton was effectively bottling up Mikan, kept the Lakers from making a rout of the game.

As they had a year earlier, the 'Trotters came out for the last half loose and inspired. Mikan scored once more to put the Lakers ahead, 26-18. Then the 'Trotters caught fire. Tatum and Haynes led the way with a barrage of incredible passes and shots. The 'Trotters scored 12 straight points and, after allowing Minneapolis a free throw, scored six more points. When the third quarter ended the Globetrotters had a 41-32 lead.

By now the Lakers were a bewildered ball club. The rout continued in the fourth quarter as Goose Tatum (who finished with 14 points), Haynes and Clifton (with 11 each) maintained their hot scoring. The tally was 47-36, when the 'Trotters decided they had reached the long-awaited moment. It was time to play for laughs.

Before the game Laker fans had boasted that the 'Trotter "voodoo stuff" would certainly not make a monkey out of Mikan. Now the star center found himself guarding Roscoe "Duke" Cumberland, one of the wildest 'Trotters. "Now you see it, now you don't," chanted Cumberland, swinging the ball around his hips and then from hand to hand in a series of lightning motions. Suddenly, Mikan *didn't*

Sweetwater Clifton passes over Mikan in the 'Trotters' second game with the Lakers.

see it. The crowd roared with laughter, for Mikan had been fooled by one of the oldest 'Trotter tricks. Cumberland had gently placed the ball on top of the dazed center's head. Before Mikan could snatch it away, another 'Trotter sneaked up from behind and recaptured it.

Next the ball went to Haynes. As the other 'Trotters sat down to rest, Marques took on the entire Laker team with his dribbling. Running, sliding, sprawling all over the floor, he kept the ball under perfect control, eluding the frustrated Lakers for over a minute. Needless to say, the crowd was hysterical. They were having as much fun as the Globetrotters.

Now, with the Lakers completely flustered, the 'Trotters went through their various comic routines, such as drop-kicking the ball from a football formation. Although the clowning enabled Minneapolis to whittle away at the score, it was too late. The 'Trotters won, 49-45. Mikan, closely guarded by Clifton, had managed to score only 19 points, 11 of which resulted from free throws.

The Globetrotters never again defeated an N.B.A. team. Time, integration, and the growth of the pro league have left them far behind as a competitive club. But the 'Trotters have not lost their magic with the fans and they still clown their way throughout the world, bringing laughter to the people of over 90 countries.

Decades have gone by and Tatum and Saperstein have both passed away. But no one who followed the Globetrotters will ever forget the team's most cherished moments—their victories over the champions of pro basketball, the Minneapolis Lakers.

four

A BLIZZARD OF BASKETS

February 10, 1949, was hardly the perfect evening to attend a basketball game in Philadelphia. Four inches of snow had fallen on the city. The Transport Workers Union was scheduled to halt all buses, trolleys and subways with a strike at midnight. Since many transport workers planned to leave their jobs a few hours before the strike deadline and automobile travel through the snow-clogged streets was slow, most Philadelphians decided that it was an excellent night to stay at home.

Thus, only 1,500 fans turned out to watch the Philadelphia Warriors play the Indianapolis Jets at the Arena. But those who came were richly rewarded. For when the evening was over, they had seen the finest professional exhibition of offensive basketball to occur during the first half of the 20th century.

The man who accomplished this feat was a quiet, lanky forward from the mountains of Kentucky. His name was Joe Fulks. Brown-haired and poker-faced, with a deceptively powerful body and long, dangling arms, Fulks was one of the first great scorers in modern pro ball.

Joe Fulks came from Birmingham, Kentucky, a little town on the banks of the Marshall River. When he was a little boy, Joe didn't even own a basketball. But after the local high school team had finished practicing on its outdoor court, he would spend hours tossing a tin can through the baskets. When the coach discovered who had been tearing up his nets each night, he gave Joe an old, dilapidated ball to practice with.

Fulks went on to become Kentucky's top high-school player. After his graduation, he attended tiny Murray State Teachers College, where he played one season before leaving to join the Marines in 1943. During World War II, Joe served at Guam and Iwo Jima. When he was discharged he quickly signed with the Warriors in the newly formed B.A.A.

From the start, the 6-foot 5-inch forward was the sparkplug of the Philadelphia offense. Owner-

Joe Fulks drives around an opponent for a successful lay-up.

coach Eddie Gottlieb knew that he needed a crowd-pleasing player like Fulks to attract fans during the first year of the franchise. So he told the other Warriors that their main job was "to get the ball to Joe."

Gottlieb's tactics were a success and fans all over the league rushed to see the high-scoring forward. Philadelphia finished second in the Eastern division during the regular season and went on to win the B.A.A. championship play-offs. Fulks led the league in scoring with 1,389 points for an average of 23.2 per game. He had 463 points more than his closest competitor in the race for the scoring title.

Fulks was far from being an all-around player and he was often criticized by sportswriters and opposing coaches. Yet few denied his value to the Warriors. "Fulks is slow and he's not a great defensive player. And how can he be a great team player when he takes so many shots?" Coach John "Honey" Russell of the Boston Celtics once said. Then Russell paused and sighed, "But I wish I had him. I'd sure build my team around him."

The Philadelphia fans cared little about Fulks's weaknesses. Joe Fulks put the ball in the basket— and that was all they asked of him.

In the 1947-48 season, when Philadelphia took first place and then lost to Baltimore in the final play-offs, Fulks again had the highest average in the league. But, because injuries had caused him to miss five games, he dropped to second place in total points, just 58 behind the leading scorer.

Then, during the 1948-49 season, Philadelphia fell into a slump. The Warriors were struggling to hold onto fourth place and get into the play-offs. Fulks's scoring rampage continued, but he found many of his records threatened by George Mikan, the Minneapolis Lakers' towering, 6-foot 10-inch center. Earlier in the season Mikan had set a new B.A.A. record by scoring 48 points against Washington. To add to his troubles, Fulks had been suffering from a stomach ailment for almost two weeks and his scoring had fallen off, creating serious problems for the Warriors.

As a result, Philadelphia was anticipating a difficult game when Indianapolis invaded the Arena that wintery night. Earlier, the Jets had handed the Warriors their worst defeat in months by clobbering them, 90-73, and they were obviously fired up for another victory. But, as it turned out, their enthusiasm was not enough to carry them through the evening. For, from the moment the game began, it was clear that something special was happening— Joe Fulks was unstoppable. Never had his touch seemed so flawless. Driving in for lay-ups and sinking his turn-around jump shot from the pivot, Fulks scored on six of his first nine attempts. Although the aroused Jets tied the score four times in the opening minutes, the first quarter ended with Philadelphia leading, 23-14.

The teams battled almost evenly through the second quarter. But Indianapolis could find no way to handle Fulks. Joe kept hitting—and the crowd loved it.

In high school Fulks had been criticized by his

coach for taking such "crazy shots" as his turn-around jumper and for transferring the ball from one hand to the other while he was in the air. "What's the matter with these shots?" he would always ask. "They go in, don't they?—and they count two points each." Joe had kept practicing these unorthodox tactics secretly. Now his determination was paying off.

He fired in spinning one-handers, running shots with either hand, overhead jumpers, driving lay-ups, tap-ins and two-handed set shots. His long fingers floated the ball softly toward the hoop, allowing it to hang on the rim and drop in even if it didn't go through cleanly.

By half time Joe had 30 points. Thirteen of his 25 shots had gone in and the Warriors led, 49-38. He hadn't missed two consecutive shots until late in the second quarter.

Philadelphia turned the contest into a rout in the last half. But the fans hardly noticed because all eyes were on Fulks. By now everyone knew that he was going after George Mikan's record of 48 points. And Indianapolis was trying hard to stop him. Coach Burl Friddle had opened the game with Carlisle Towery guarding Fulks. By the time it was over, Price Brookfield, John Mandic, Leo Mogus and Jack Eskridge had been given the assignment. But each man failed.

During his record-breaking performance against the Indianapolis Jets, Fulks (10) tries to snare a loose ball.

Late in the third quarter Joe hit three straight baskets. Soon after, he tapped in a missed foul shot to raise his total to 47 points. The tiny crowd screamed so loudly that it seemed the Arena was packed.

With a minute and 50 seconds to go in the quarter, Fulks leaped over two Jets to grab an offensive rebound. As the defenders pawed hopelessly at the air, he whirled and swished in a short, one-handed jumper. Fulks had 49 points. Mikan's record was broken.

The third quarter ended with Philadelphia leading, 77-70. Fulks had connected on 21 of 40 shots from the field. But Joe's stomach problems had left him weak and he was tiring quickly. In the fourth quarter, however, the points kept coming. Coach Friddle was so exasperated by his team's inability to stop Fulks that he jokingly sent one of his own players into the game as a substitute for "Jumpin' Joe." But Fulks just laughed and sent the "substitute" back to the Indianapolis bench.

With victory already assured, the Warriors' coach, Eddie Gottlieb, instructed his players to concentrate even more than usual on getting the ball to Fulks. As it turned out, the Warriors were so unselfish that Fulks finished the game with three more shots than the rest of the Philadelphia team combined.

As exhaustion swept over him, Fulks's shooting accuracy fell off, but not by much. The points kept coming. With four minutes left in the game, he dropped in a set shot to give him 59 points. The crowd began to yell for 60. Fulks summoned all his strength for one final burst.

Indianapolis missed a shot and the Warriors were off on a fast break. Francis "Chink" Crossin hit Fulks with a quick pass. Joe drove in for an easy lay-up. He had 61 points.

Then, as the clock ticked away and the Jets' defense surrounded him, Fulks dribbled into the corner and shot again. His twisting, jumping two-hander was good. Fulks had scored 63 points. But he was too tired to continue. There were 56 seconds left when Coach Gottlieb sent in a substitute. His teammates mobbed Fulks as he came back to the bench. The crowd echoed his name throughout the half-empty Arena. Even Burl Friddle, the opposing coach, turned his back on the game to shake Joe's hand.

The final score was 108-87. It hardly mattered, for Fulks had set league records for points in a half (33), shots attempted (56), and field goals scored (27). Most important, at a time when entire pro teams were sometimes held to fewer than 60 points, "Jumpin' Joe" Fulks had scored 63 points—a record that would last for 10 years.

five

COUSY WORKS OVERTIME

Even though it is hard to believe, there was a time when Bob Cousy and the Boston Celtics were not synonymous with success in professional basketball. In fact, for a while, the Celtics didn't think very much of Cousy and nobody thought very much of the Celtics.

Cousy went on to become the cleverest playmaker in the N.B.A., but when the fancy-passing guard was graduated from Holy Cross in 1950, Red Auerbach, the Celtics' new coach, turned down the opportunity to draft him. Boston had finished last the previous season and, according to the rules of the college draft, the Celtics would have first choice of all the eligible players. Auerbach wanted a big man and, although Cousy was a local hero and an

All-American, Red thought he was too small and that his behind-the-back passes would never succeed in pro ball.

Auerbach was not a particularly tactful man and he didn't hesitate to tell the Boston press what he thought of their star collegian. At a press conference, when the writers asked him why he wasn't drafting Cousy, the blustery coach turned

Cousy at Holy Cross

to Celtics owner Walter Brown and snapped: "Am I supposed to win or am I supposed to worry about the local yokels?"

Thus, Boston never drafted Bob Cousy. But the Celtics got him in spite of themselves—before he ever played a pro game. It happened because the B.A.A. and the N.B.L. merged in 1949-50, leaving an unwieldly, three-division, 17-team N.B.A. Shortly after the season ended, a number of midwest clubs went into bankruptcy and folded. As a result, their players were put into a pool to be drafted by the remaining clubs. Although Cousy had no pro experience, he was placed in a special draft with two of the N.B.A.'s top guards, Max Zaslofsky and Andy Phillip. Then, much to their chagrin, the Celtics pulled Cousy's name out of a hat. It turned out to be the luckiest thing that ever happened to basketball in Boston.

The Celtics of the early 1950s were swift, high-scoring clubs. But they were weak on defense and rebounding and in Cousy's first two seasons they were eliminated in the first round of the N.B.A. play-offs. However, Cousy was an immediate hit with the Boston fans. In those first two years he averaged 15.6 and 21.7 points per game and dazzled the crowd with his sleight-of-hand passing.

But Auerbach still wasn't convinced of Cousy's ability. He later recalled: "Cousy wasn't that good his first couple of seasons. . . . He'd make the plays, but he'd lose the ball a lot."

During the 1952-53 season, owner Walter Brown even chastised Cousy at a Basketball Writers' Luncheon. The previous evening, the Celtics had been clobbered by the Warriors. Cousy, by now Boston's top-salaried man, had scored only four points. "That's a lot of money per point," Brown snapped. "I don't need an expensive club to lose. I can lose just as easily with a cheap one."

By the time Cousy heard the story it had been distorted so much that it seemed as though Brown wanted to trade him. Cousy, a sensitive young man, was hurt. "If the Celtics aren't satisfied with my playing," he exploded, "I want to be traded."

Brown hurriedly apologized. If he hadn't, the Celtics might have followed such franchises as the Anderson Packers and Sheboygan Redskins into the graveyard of professional basketball. More than any individual, Cousy, a David in a game of Goliaths, popularized the pro sport in Boston and throughout the nation. And during the 1952-53 season "The Magician of the Hardcourt" truly came into his own.

However, in spite of Cousy's brilliant playmaking, the Celtics were struggling to stay near the top. On the final day of the regular season, Auerbach's club defeated the Baltimore Bullets, 92-78, to tie

Syracuse for second place. The tie was broken in an extra game at Syracuse and Boston lost, 72-68.

In the opening round of the postseason play-offs, the Celtics and Nationals would meet again. If past experience meant anything, there was little hope for Boston. Auerbach's teams had reached the play-offs each of his five years in pro ball, but only once had they gotten past the first round. Even worse, since Syracuse had finished second that year, the Nats would have the home-court advantage in the first and third games of the "best-of-three" series. It was a big advantage, for over the past four years Boston had lost 13 of 14 games played in Syracuse.

However, the Nats were in for a surprise. In Syracuse, the Celtics hit 28 foul shots in the final quarter and upset the Nationals, 87-81.

But the Celtics had to win again—and they knew they had to do it in Boston. To add to their problems, the Celtics were suffering from injuries. Muscleman Bob Brannum had a twisted ankle and Cousy had twisted his knee. Many doubted that Cousy could maneuver at top speed. But that day, he surprised everyone and put on an incredible performance in one of the longest, wildest basketball games ever played.

From the start, the body contact between the teams was ferocious. Syracuse's star, the 6-foot 8-

inch forward, Dolph Schayes controlled the boards, and the Nats jumped to an 8-0 lead. But Cousy's passing helped cut the margin to 22-21 by the end of the first period. Then, with 8 minutes and 13 seconds left in the half and Syracuse ahead, 29-27, the game turned into a brawl. Brannum, whose reputation as a rough player was well known throughout the league, had been dogging Schayes closely. Suddenly the two collided and Dolph hit the floor near the Nats' bench. Moments later Schayes bumped Brannum hard under the Celtics' basket. Brannum shoved back and Schayes promptly hit him in the eye with a solid punch. Then Brannum belted Schayes. Players, fans, and police poured onto the court. When order was restored, both Schayes and Brannum were thrown out of the game. Syracuse argued that the wily Auerbach had sent Brannum in to provoke a fight with its star. But the protest made no difference. Schayes remained out of the game.

In spite of the handicap, Syracuse refused to quit. The rough-and-tumble contest became a parade to the foul line, and the Nationals left the floor at half time with a 42-40 lead. Cousy had scored only seven points.

The last half was just as close and hard-fought. At the end of the third quarter, Boston led, 62-59. Cousy was beginning to hit with drives and one-handers. During the final quarter, the tension began to build as the lead shifted back and forth. The Celtics were unable to gain a decisive advantage. Their deadly accuracy from the foul line, plus Ed Macauley's close shots and Cousy's outside bombs, were being effectively counteracted by Syracuse's balanced offense.

In the closing moments Syracuse took the lead, 77-76. The excitement mounted as Cooz dribbled around the foul circle and then tried to hit Macauley with a quick pass. The crowd groaned as the pass went wild and Syracuse took possession of the ball. The Celtics were on the verge of defeat and Cousy would be blamed if they lost.

If Syracuse could stall out the final seconds it would win. But somehow Boston stole the ball. Quickly the Celtics worked it to Cousy, who was promptly fouled. He had to make his free throw. The crowd of 11,058 fans held their breath as Bob bounced the ball and took aim. The shot swished through the net to tie the score at 77-77, sending the game into overtime.

From then on it was Bob Cousy against Syracuse. He hit a pair of foul shots to give Boston an 84-82 lead. But Syracuse kept fighting back. In the closing seconds Cousy again found himself at the line with Boston behind by one point. An eerie silence fell over Boston Garden. Again Cousy hit his foul

Cousy drives through two Nats opponents to score.

shot. The first overtime ended with a score of 86-86. Bob had scored six of his team's nine points during that period.

The pressure mounted in the second overtime. Each team maneuvered the ball carefully because neither could afford a bad shot. Soon the Nats led, 90-88. Time was running out and it was up to Cousy once more. Bob drove, his huge hands and long arms deftly controlling the dribble. As the Syracuse defense began to converge around the hoop, Cousy stopped short and lofted a one-handed jumper. The ball went in cleanly to tie the score, 90-90, and send the game into another overtime.

Now both teams were in serious trouble because so many players had fouled out of the game. Syracuse, in fact, had no eligible players left on its bench when the third overtime started. Then, with the score tied at 93-93, the Nats' Seymour aggravated a month-old leg injury. Player-coach Al Cervi faced a hard choice. If he put in a substitute, Syracuse would lose the ball and be slapped with a technical foul for using an ineligible player. If he left Seymour in, Boston would actually have a one-man advantage. Cervi decided to gamble on Seymour, stationing him under the defensive basket.

Even with four men the Nats' offense clicked. Slowly Syracuse's lead mounted. With 18 seconds remaining the Nationals led, 99-94. The Celtics seemed beaten and their downcast fans began to head toward the exits. But they hadn't counted on Cousy.

The indomitable Celtic drove for the basket and shot just as he was knocked to the floor by one of the Syracuse defenders. Somehow, the ball went in. In addition, Cousy had a foul shot coming. He made it and the Nats' lead was reduced to two points.

Syracuse came downcourt, but the Celtics stole the ball with five seconds left. Racing the clock, Cousy dribbled across midcourt and arched a 25-foot one-hander. The buzzer sounded with the ball still in the air. But the shot was good and the score stood at 99-99. Cousy had scored eight of Boston's nine points in the third overtime. And now the two teams would play a fourth.

The tension was too much for owner Walter Brown. He left his front-row seat and watched the remainder of the game on a TV set in his office. Up in the press box, the Celtics' public relations man, Howie McHugh, passed out. The fans were hoarse from screaming.

Again Syracuse pulled ahead. Then, with no substitutes left on the Boston bench, Chuck Cooper committed his sixth personal foul. Cooper was permitted to remain in the game, but it cost Boston a technical foul in addition to the personal foul. Syracuse hit both free throws and then slapped in a rebound to lead, 104-99.

Tired and slowed by his injured leg, Cousy brought the Celtics back one last time. He hit a foul shot and followed with two field goals. The game was tied for the 26th and final time.

After that Cousy's teammates chipped in. With less than two minutes remaining, John Mahnken hit a foul shot and Ken Rollins hit another to give the Celtics a 106-104 lead.

Cervi drove and was fouled in the act of shooting. His first shot was good. The second bounced off the rim and Boston grabbed the rebound. Celtic fans began to sense victory.

Cousy started to dribble, running out the clock. Syracuse tried frantically to steal the ball, but Cooz kept dribbling. Finally, the Nats were forced to foul, hoping the Celtics would miss their free throws. But Cooz hit three of four and Cooper also sank a pair. At last the time ran out and the game was over. Boston had won, 111-105, in four overtimes. There had been 106 fouls in the game. Cousy had hit 10 of 18 shots from the floor, an unprecedented 30 of 32 from the foul line and had set a play-off record with 50 points—25 in overtime.

In the Nats' silent locker room, Cervi sadly shook his head. "He did it," the coach mumbled. "Just that one kid. We should be going back to Syracuse to play a third game. Instead we're going home for the year. What a player! He's the best."

At the same moment, in Boston's boisterous quarters, Cousy sat before his locker exhausted, his head buried in his hands. "I can't believe it's over," he gasped. "I can't believe it's over."

Walter Brown, who had seen the final minutes on TV, was thankful it was over, too. "The greatest individual performance I've ever ever seen," said the Celtic's owner.

And from across the room teammate Bob Harris cried, "Mr. Brown, Mr. Brown, how'd you like that? How'd you like that? Let's face it—once and for all. There's nobody anywhere like that Cooz!"

Boston lost in the next round of the play-offs that year. But the basketball world had seen a preview of what was ahead for Bob Cousy and the Celtics.

six

THE GREATEST ALL-STAR GAME

The night of the 1954 East-West All-Star game at Madison Square Garden, the New York Knickerbockers' Joe Lapchick, coach of the East, walked into his team's dressing room and stopped short. Even though he had seen the players in pregame warm-ups, his mouth fell open as he looked around the room. Seated in front of the lockers was Boston's brilliant backcourt combination—the magic-fingered Bob Cousy and Bill Sharman, the most feared outside shooter in the sport. Nearby sat Philadelphia's lanky Neil Johnston, the leading scorer in the N.B.A., and New York's Harry "The Horse" Gallatin, the top rebounder in the league.

Standing against one wall were Lapchick's own

great guards, Carl Braun, a deadly two-handed set-shooter, and "Tricky Dick" McGuire, Cousy's closest rival as a playmaker. Slowly, Lapchick's eyes focused on the other men in the room: Dolph Schayes of Syracuse, the best forward in the game; "Easy" Ed Macauley, Boston's scoring ace; Paul Seymour, the Syracuse Nats' star guard; and Baltimore's towering Ray Felix, well on his way to Rookie-of-the-Year honors. Nine of the N.B.A.'s 11 leading scorers were gathered in one room!

"I was scared to death when I walked in there," Lapchick recalls. "I sort of gasped. I'd never seen so many tremendous players before. What plays could I give them? What advice could I offer? I felt helpless. Finally I cleared my throat, stammered a bit and then made the best dressing room speech of my life. 'Let's go fellows,' I said. That was all."

And that was all that seemed necessary, for the East had speed, size and superior scoring punch. Of the three previous All-Star games the East had won two and was a solid favorite to win this year, also.

The West, led by Minneapolis' already legendary center, 6-foot 10-inch George Mikan, was hardly considered a pushover, though. Its forwards included Mikan's rugged teammate, Jim Pollard, Milwaukee's leaping Mel Hutchins and big Arnie

Risen of Rochester. Bob Davies and Bobby Wanzer, Rochester's quick and dangerous guards, were ready for backcourt duty, along with the Lakers' great Slater Martin. Larry Foust of Fort Wayne, the N.B.A.'s third-ranking rebounder, was available to relieve Mikan. It was a good team, but the East had a great one.

Hopes weren't running very high in the Western camp on the day of the game. So Milwaukee's volatile owner, Ben Kerner, decided that it might help if he gave the East a little needling. At a pre-game luncheon he gestured across the table to the East's stars and chided, "Look at them. They're mad at Cousy already. He won't even pass the butter, much less the basketball!"

The players just grinned, however, for Cousy was the greatest passer in pro basketball. It would take more than Kerner's jibes to unsettle them.

But when the game began, the East ran into unexpected difficulty. Jim Pollard fired in three quick baskets and, as a crowd of 16,487 watched in disbelief, the West raced to a 9-0 lead.

The East kept its composure, though. Lapchick had gambled by starting Felix, a rookie, ahead of the high-scoring Neil Johnston. His gamble seemed justified when Felix caused Mikan to commit three quick fouls. Then Felix and Macauley began taking the initiative around the basket. The

The West's Andy Phillip (4) leaps high to take a rebound from the East's Carl Braun.

East tied the score at 13-13 and led at the end of the first quarter, 28-25.

In the second quarter the Easterners showed why even Lapchick, an Original Celtic who had seen great players for almost half a century, held them in awe. Cousy and McGuire dazzled the crowd— and the West's defense—with their ball handling. Cousy, flashy and exciting, whipped passes behind his back, and the steady McGuire threaded the ball through the defense. "They were passing the ball around so fast I had trouble following it," raved the Knicks' Carl Braun after the game.

But the West hung on. Davies began hitting from outside and Pollard continued to score from the corner. They tied the score at 44-44, only to see a pair of foul shots by Gallatin and a last-second one-hander by Sharman send the East into the locker room at half time with a 48-44 lead.

The bruising, seesaw battle continued throughout the last half. Cousy and McGuire kept up their ballhandling wizardry, but the East's attack bogged down when Felix went to the bench because of foul trouble. The West's coach, John Kundla, kept the pressure on by using Mikan and the 6-foot 9-inch, 250-pound Foust under the boards at the same time. Mikan was scoring now and the crowd sensed an upset. The West led at the end of the third quarter, 67-65.

The final quarter was a maelstrom of fast, furious action. Mikan, Foust, Gallatin and Schayes crashed together time after time as they battled for rebounds. Meanwhile, in the backcourt, Davies and Wanzer were fighting to a stand-off against the East's great guards.

As the clock raced on, the East scrambled into the lead. With just 35 seconds of playing time left,

The West's George Mikan contends with Neil Johnston for the ball.

the score was 82-80 and the East had possession of the ball.

Lapchick looked down his bench and signaled to Cousy, who had been taking a quick breather. It was time for "the Cooz" to do what he did best—dribble out the clock. (At the time there was no rule requiring a team to shoot the ball within 24 seconds.) As he reported into the game the West seemed doomed. If they couldn't steal the ball they were finished.

The crowd was standing as Cooz gracefully controlled the ball in the backcourt. Then it happened. Bob Davies darted in from the side, swooped down and batted the ball from Cousy's grasp. The fans groaned as Davies scooped up the ball and drove in unmolested to tie the score, 82-82.

But Cousy was unruffled and he soon got his chance for redemption. The East brought the ball upcourt, looking for one last shot. Carefully they worked it to the dead-eyed Sharman, who fired a one-hander toward the basket. But the shot was wide to the left. Gallatin muscled his way through a swarm of players under the boards, ripped the ball from the hands of a Western rebounder and passed it back to Cousy. Cool as an iceberg, Cooz sank a 20-foot set shot. The crowd exploded with cheers. The East led, 84-82, and there were just six seconds left.

But this was just the sort of pressure that the West's Mikan relished. The ball was passed to Davies, who hurriedly called time out, giving the West possession at midcourt. Now there were only three seconds left. The obvious strategy was to set Mikan up for one last shot. From midcourt, Pollard passed to Davies, who whipped the ball to Mikan. The bespectacled center whirled for his jump shot, but was hit on the arm by Felix just as the buzzer sounded. Although there was no time left on the clock, Mikan was given two free throws because of Felix's foul. He had to score on both to send the game into overtime. The court was cleared of players, leaving Mikan all alone with the pressure.

Madison Square Garden was a madhouse. Every person was standing and screaming, yet Mikan seemed oblivious to the ear-splitting noise. Finally, as he toed the free-throw line, the shouts of the crowd dwindled to a bubbling murmur of anticipation. Sid Borgia, the referee, spun the ball on his fingertips and stared at Mikan, who had heckled and bedeviled Borgia over the years. This was an opportunity Borgia found impossible to resist.

"Remember how you've always needled me and accused me of choking up in the clutch?" asked Borgia.

"Deservedly, too," said Mikan, grinning at him.

(Above) Cousy takes a pass while being guarded by the West's Bob Wanzer. (Below) Joe Lapchick with his 1954 All-Star team after their victory.

"Well, let's see who chokes now," said Borgia triumphantly. He handed the ball to Mikan, who was still grinning. Mikan bounced the ball at the line a couple of times, smiled and calmly made the first shot. Then he stepped away from the line. While the fans tried to unnerve him with their partisan uproar, Mikan walked around the court grinning until he was good and ready. Then he stepped back to the line. Smiling again at Borgia, he bounced the ball a couple of times. And then— swish! The game was now in overtime. There was a momentary lull. Then the crowd, who moments earlier had jeered Mikan, broke into one of the greatest ovations in the history of the Garden. For every person realized the incredible pressure Mikan had just conquered.

It seemed impossible that anyone could supply an encore to such a dramatic moment, but Cousy managed to do just that. He turned the overtime into a one-man show as he scored 10 of the East's 14 points and controlled the ball with an unforgettable exhibition of dribbling.

Cooz quickly put the East ahead with a long set-shot. A minute later, Sharman made a three-point play that pushed the East's lead to 90-86. The rest of the game belonged to Cousy. He dribbled all over the court as two and three Western defenders tried frantically to steal the ball. But Cousy did not intend to lose it again. Finally, in total frustration, the West began to foul him. But that was a suicidal tactic, for Cousy proceeded to make six straight free throws. He tossed in another basket for good measure and, as the clock ticked away, he danced around with his elusive, bewildering dribble. Then it was all over. The East had won, 98-93.

There was a curious sidenote to the game. In the traditional polling of the press just before the end of the regulation game, the West's Pollard had been voted the Most Valuable Player in the game. But after Cousy's heroics, another vote was taken and, not surprisingly, the Celtics' star won. Pollard still led all scorers with 23 points and Cousy topped the East with 20. Mikan? He had 18, and there wasn't a person in the crowd who would ever forget his two free throws that night. Nor would they forget Cousy's performance. As the jubilant Eastern players trooped into their locker room, New York's Carl Braun, his hand outstretched, went up to Cousy and said, "Cooz, the greatest is still the greatest."

seven

THE LAKERS' LAST HURRAH

The early years of the N.B.A. belonged to the Minneapolis Lakers. They were the monarchs of professional basketball. The league was their kingdom and they ruled it with an iron hand. No team—not even the Original Celtics—had ever dominated the sport so completely.

The Lakers' dynasty began in 1947-48 with the arrival of George Mikan, the first pro to combine great height with great skill. Mikan was 6 feet 10 inches tall and weighed 245 pounds. But he was no freak. Unlike most big men of his time, Mikan was graceful as well as strong, a fine shooter as well as a tenacious rebounder.

After winning All-America honors at De Paul University, Mikan began his pro career in the

George Mikan

1946-47 season with the Chicago Gears of the National Basketball League. Although he was among the league's leaders in scoring, the Gears folded at the end of the season. Mikan then joined the new N.B.L. franchise in Minneapolis—and the Lakers rolled to the championship in 1947-48.

The rival Basketball Association of America (soon to become the N.B.A.) had no chance to get

Mikan in a trade, so they did the next best thing. They talked Minneapolis into joining their league. That was like letting the fox in with the chickens— except that, while losing to Mikan, every team made money. For "Big George" was the greatest drawing card and the highest-salaried player in the sport.

Mikan and the Lakers quickly established themselves as the dominant force in the N.B.A. After finishing half a game behind Rochester in the Western division, they swept aside Chicago, Rochester and Washington to win the play-offs. Mikan, who tallied over 30 points in 25 games, led the league in scoring with a record 28.3 average.

But Mikan was not the whole team. Laker coach John Kundla had another ace: Jim Pollard, a smooth, lanky 6-foot 5-inch forward from Stanford. Pollard had been with the Lakers from the start and he worked perfectly with Mikan under the boards. Together they made Minneapolis unstoppable around the basket.

The following season, 1949-50, the Lakers added two more stars. Vern Mikkelsen of Hamline University, a rugged 6-foot 8-inch forward, teamed with Mikan and Pollard to give the Lakers a matchless front line. Vern was a good shot and his rebounding and defense were brilliant.

The other vital newcomer was Slater Martin, a

fiery 5-foot 10-inch guard from the University of
Texas. Martin seemed small enough to fit in Mikan's
pocket. But he was an excellent ball-handler, who
gave direction and cohesion to the Lakers' attack.
A solid, aggressive defensive player, Martin didn't
shoot much, but he could score when he had to.

The nucleus of the dynasty had been formed and
the Lakers began to pick up more momentum. In
1949-50 Mikan again led the league in scoring
(27.4) while Pollard (14.7) and Mikkelsen (11.6)

Vern Mikkelsen tries to block a shot by Bob Pettit.

also averaged in double figures. Minneapolis won the division championship and roared to another play-off victory, beating the Syracuse Nationals in the finals, four games to two.

By now Mikan was the N.B.A.'s most exciting superstar. No one could outmuscle him under the boards. But Mikan, an intelligent man who was studying to become a lawyer, absorbed great punishment in the process. Once, after a rough game in New York, a reporter walked into the Lakers' dressing room and told the exhausted Mikan that the Knicks had accused him of illegally elbowing them. Mikan peeled off his jersey and showed the surprised reporter his torso, which was literally crisscrossed with black-and-blue welts. "Ask them what they think these are," Mikan snapped. "Birthmarks?"

In the six seasons from 1947 to 1953 Big George led Minneapolis to five championships. With such a successful record the Lakers saw little reason to change their strategy. Their offense still revolved around Mikan. They would bring the ball up the court slowly to give their lumbering center time to move into position under the basket. Then the guards would pass to him and Mikan would either maneuver for a shot or (especially if he was double-teamed) pass off to one of the forwards. The strategy was simple and incredibly effective. When the outspoken Martin complained that such a ponderous attack seldom gave him a chance to display his talent, a Laker official snapped, "We can win with Mikan, Pollard, Mikkelsen and two bellhops. Who needs you?"

By 1953-54, such internal problems had begun to hamper the perennial champs and it was not a very happy season for the Lakers. First, Martin was displeased with his contract. Then Pollard and Mikan argued openly during a game. Mikan accused his teammates of deliberately withholding the ball and using him as a decoy.

But Kundla managed to pull the team back together just in time to defend its position atop the basketball world. Finishing with a rush, the Lakers captured the Western division title by two games and went on to defeat Fort Wayne and Rochester in the initial rounds of the play-offs.

By now, however, Mikan had slowed down considerably. Although he was still one of the most feared and effective players in the game, he had averaged a relatively low 18.1 points per game during the regular season. Many people were convinced that he would retire after the play-offs. (Mikan did retire, but he returned for a short while in 1956.)

The Lakers, nevertheless, were heavy favorites in the play-off finals. Their opponents, the Syracuse

Jim Pollard bats the ball away from a Knickerbocker opponent.

Nationals, were the Cinderella team of the Eastern division. The Nats had tied for second place during the regular season, then upset New York and Boston in the play-offs. Syracuse, however, entered the finals with an injury-riddled team. Dolph Schayes, the club's leading scorer and rebounder, had a broken wrist and Earl Lloyd, their 6-foot 6-inch center, had a broken hand. Both were forced to play wearing casts. Without the excellent rebounding they usually supplied, the Nationals' feared fast break was not expected to get rolling. Increasing the odds against Syracuse was the fact that the Lakers had a tradition to defend—and they were always at their best in the play-offs.

But the Lakers knew they would have a struggle on their hands. They were not quite the great team that had won the title so many times before. They were slower and older now and the players seemed to realize that their dynasty was coming to an end. The next season a new rule, forcing a team to shoot within 24 seconds, would be in effect. This would hurt slow-moving clubs like Minneapolis. For awhile, at least, this would be the Lakers' last shot at a title.

During the first game the Lakers appeared lethargic and the Nats' fast break turned out to give them more trouble than was expected. They managed to salvage the game only after Kundla sent rookie Clyde Lovellette into the line-up. Teaming with Mikan under the boards, the hayseed from the University of Kansas scored 16 points. Mikan scored 15 and the Lakers rallied to win, 79-68.

But Coach Kundla was worried. "Everybody thinks we should beat Syracuse by 20 points just because they're injured," he said before the second game. "But they're not going to quit because of that. They've got a lot of fight and hustle left. Yet, because they're hurt, *we* don't seem to have the spirit we should."

He was right, for in the next game the Lakers' performance was just as uninspired. With 30 seconds remaining, the Nationals led, 60-58. The Lakers brought the ball up the court slowly. As usual, they were looking for Mikan. And this time they found him. Big George slipped loose from his coverage, grabbed a pass from Jim Holstein and dunked the ball with a flourish. The home crowd roared with glee. The score was 60-60, and there were only 18 seconds left to play. Now the Lakers were sure they could pull the game out of the fire.

Paul Seymour, the Nats' veteran guard, hurriedly dribbled upcourt. Syracuse's plan was to maneuver the ball inside for a close shot. But the Lakers were expecting that. So, when Seymour saw the Minneapolis defense drop back, he shocked everyone in the building, including his teammates, by casting off a 45-foot set shot.

The ball rose high in the air toward the basket. The Lakers watched, open-mouthed and unbelieving, as it swished through the hoop to bring the score to 62-60. They were so disconcerted that they couldn't get off another shot and Syracuse won. It was the first time in the Lakers' history that they had lost a play-off game on their home court.

Needless to say, the sudden, dramatic victory

gave the Nats momentum. In addition, the next three games would be played in Syracuse, where the eastern team would have the advantage of playing on its home court.

Then, in the third game, Mikan reminded the basketball world that he was still one of the greatest players in the game. Just as he had been doing for seven years, he lifted the Lakers when they needed it most. Overpowering the opposition under the basket, tapping in rebounds and banking hook shots off the boards, Mikan scored 12 points in the first quarter and the Lakers leaped to a 24-16 lead.

Although the Nats were decimated by injuries, they refused to concede. With the half almost over, they tied the score, 31-31. Then Mikan exploded again. Three sweeping rebounds, a savage dunk and a soft hook-shot sent Minneapolis to the locker room ahead.

Syracuse made another threatening move early in the third quarter, cutting the lead to 43-40. But Mikan broke the game open with a devastating display of power, making three straight three-point plays.

Despite the angry hooting of the Syracuse crowd, Mikan contributed 30 points and 15 rebounds to the Lakers' 81-67 victory. "I can't remember when George played so well," marveled Coach Kundla.

"He certainly came up with a big game at the right moment."

Now the pressure was on Syracuse. Schayes had scored just five points in the first three games. In contrast, Mikan was hot. And before the fourth game it was revealed that the Nats' fine guard, George King, had cracked a bone in his wrist and would also have to play with a cast.

Dolph Schayes, with a lightweight cast on his left wrist, shoots over Pollard and Mikan.

With three men slowed down by playing in casts, the Nats decided to gamble. They fit Schayes with a new, lightweight cast—and hoped that his wrist would be adequately protected. Schayes liked it. "It feels like part of my arm," he said. "I feel much more loose and comfortable."

He made the Nats feel loose and comfortable, too, scoring 10 points and combining with Osterkorn and Bob Lavoy to hold Mikan to only 12. Seymour bombed in 25 points from the outside and the Nationals evened the series, two games apiece, by upsetting Minneapolis, 80-69.

Disgusted by their performance against a crippled opponent, the Lakers resorted to raw power and routed the Nats in the fifth game. In the first quarter Mikan rammed in 10 points, giving the Lakers a 22-17 lead. Then Lovellete replaced Mikan in the pivot and took over where the tired veteran had left off. The 6-foot 9-inch rookie scored 11 points in the second quarter.

In the last half Martin's passes to Mikkelsen kept the Lakers rolling. Mikkelsen didn't miss often and finished with 21 points. Mikan and Lovellette had 14 each. Minneapolis won easily, 84-73. They were one victory away from another title.

The Lakers talked confidently of "winning in six" as they flew back to Minneapolis. They were playing well again and the Nats were so battered that only one man on their roster, substitute Al Masino, was not using some sort of cast or heavy bandage.

The crowd at the Minneapolis Auditorium went wild in the first quarter as the Lakers appeared to break the sixth game open. Mikan put on a stunning display of power, using his bulk around the basket to hit lay-ups and tap-in's. The huge center scored 17 points and Minneapolis opened up a 27-19 lead.

But the dogged Nats rallied once more. They cut the lead to 43-38 by half time, and then turned on a savage defense in the third quarter. At that point the Lakers began to make wild passes and take bad shots and by the end of the third quarter Syracuse led, 54-49. Laker fans couldn't believe their eyes. The most powerful team in pro basketball had scored only six points in an entire quarter. Even worse, they had managed but one point in the last nine minutes.

Minneapolis' shooting wasn't much better in the fourth quarter. But the Nationals weren't hitting, either, and the Lakers narrowed the lead. With 2 minutes and 3 seconds remaining in the game, Pollard coolly sank a pair of foul shots to tie the score, 63-63. The Lakers were on the verge of victory.

Syracuse was able to stall for one last shot. With 30 seconds left the Nats called time-out. Schayes had already fouled out of the game, so Syracuse had to find someone else to try the final shot.

Schayes had an idea. "Get Neal in the line-up," he said to player-coach Al Cervi. "Let him shoot."

Ebberle "Jim" Neal was a seldom-used, 6-foot 11-inch center from South Carolina. He played rarely because he was a rookie and had averaged just 4.7 a game. But Neal did have a good hook shot. Cervi agreed with Schayes. "Okay, Neal," he said. "Get in there and hit the hook shot or draw a foul."

As the clock ticked away, Seymour dribbled the ball. Then he fired a quick pass to Neal in the pivot. But the tall Southerner was so nervous that the ball bounced off his hands. Seymour raced in, scooped up the ball and fed it to Neal again. This time the rookie was too far from the basket to try his hook shot.

At last, in desperation, Neal turned and threw an off-balance, 25-foot one-hander toward the basket. The ball dropped through without touching the rim. Syracuse had won, 65-63. The team that was supposed to lose four in a row had pushed the vaunted Lakers to the seventh game.

The Minneapolis dressing room was silent as a tomb. The players were too ashamed to speak. Mikan, who had scored 30 points and grabbed 18 rebounds, sat with his head bowed, staring at his shoes. Martin clenched and unclenched his fists.

Pollard held his head in his hands. Finally Coach Kundla stood up and walked to the center of the room. "We've got to win now," he told them solemnly. "There's just nothing else we can do. We've just got to win."

Across the hall there was jubilation. The Nats shouted and slapped each other on the back. One more victory and they would topple the greatest dynasty in basketball history.

After his teammates had serenaded him with "Dixie," Jim Neal entertained the press. Few times, if ever, had a more obscure player hit a more important shot. And, for one night at least, Neal was a hero. "Boys," he drawled happily, "Ah'm a perfect shooter. Ah take one shot, and Ah make one basket. How about that?"

Above the noise Seymour shouted to reporters: "We've come too far to let it slip away now. We'll keep battling all the way and maybe we can force the breaks to come in our direction."

Several stalls away Dolph Schayes bit his lip nervously. He knew that the Lakers were too great to go down without a struggle. "I wish we were playing them tonight," he said quietly. "Those old pros will be rested up by tomorrow."

Schayes' fears were justified, for Minneapolis was bursting with pride and anger. After winning five championships they didn't want their reputation thrown away by a shoddy performance. The future might belong to teams like Syracuse, but the Lakers wanted one more title. This was to be Mikan's last game and the Lakers' "Last Hurrah."

The game started slowly, but a jump shot by Pollard from the corner sent Minneapolis ahead, 8-7. Mikan followed with a short hook-shot. From then on the Lakers never trailed again. They had a 17-14 lead at the quarter and increased it to 38-32 by half time. Mikan wasn't hitting, but the big man was a tower of strength under the boards. As the crowd cheered them on, he and Lovellette controlled the rebounds, limiting Syracuse to one shot at a time.

The Lakers broke the game open in the last half. Martin hit from the outside and Pollard kept swishing through jump shots from the corner. When Syracuse put pressure on him, Jim twisted through the Nats' defense for spectacular lay-ups. Late in the third quarter the Lakers led, 61-45.

Then the valiant Nationals made one final charge. Schayes, Seymour and Osterkorn went over and around the Lakers, scoring again and again. With six minutes left to play the margin had been sliced to 74-65.

Then the Lakers wrapped it up. Martin went into his fancy dribbling act, controlling the ball and forcing the Nats to foul. And after each foul Slater would sink the free throw. Mikan, who already had 15 rebounds, began to dominate the boards once more. Pollard, Martin and Mikan each stole a pass from the frantic Nationals. The Lakers' lead was now 84-70.

Moments later the game was over and the old pros had come through again. Pollard, who had played 47 exhausting minutes, had scored 21 points. Martin had 12, Mikan 11, and Mikkelsen 7. Minneapolis had out-rebounded Syracuse, 56-38. And the Lakers had won the game and the championship by a score of 87-80.

"We rose up as a team," Mikan said proudly in the locker room. "Finally everyone was 'up' for this one."

Coach John Kundla nodded his head. Around him the players were laughing and cheering. He stared fondly at the men who had won their sixth championship in seven seasons. "This is the most cherished of all the titles," Kundla said. "It's the most cherished because it was our toughest struggle. . . . It was definitely our biggest win of the last seven years."

eight

BIRTH OF A DYNASTY

During modern pro basketball's first decade (1946-1956) two teams emerged as symbols of frustration: the Boston Celtics and the St. Louis Hawks. Boston, a charter member of the N.B.A., boasted a galaxy of stars. But even with Bob Cousy, Bill Sharman and Ed Macauley, the Celtics never managed to finish first during the regular season or to win the Eastern division play-offs.

The Hawks had exasperated their owner, Ben Kerner, for 10 financially painful seasons. They had bounced from Buffalo to Tri-Cities, to Milwaukee and then, in the 1955-56 season, to St. Louis, destroying basketball interest wherever they went and never producing a winning record. In 1951-52, while embarrassing the city of Milwaukee, they actually lost 49 of 66 games.

But in 1956-57 everything changed. During that season Boston and St. Louis became seats of power in the N.B.A.—ironically, by helping each other. The Celtics had always needed a big, tough center who could play defense, rebound and launch their celebrated fast break. They got that man from St. Louis. His name was Bill Russell.

St. Louis had the draft rights to Russell, a 6-foot 9-inch rookie who had led the University of San Francisco to a pair of N.C.A.A. titles. But the Hawks were interested in a trade because Kerner wanted the Celtics' Ed Macauley. "Easy Ed" had been a star at St. Louis University and the Hawks' attendance-conscious owner was sure that Macauley would attract a large number of fans. Red Auerbach, the Celtics' boisterous coach, decided to stake his reputation and future on Russell. So Boston sent Macauley and Cliff Hagan, a rookie forward from Kentucky, to St. Louis in exchange for the untested Russell. Then Auerbach outbid the Globetrotters for the center's services and waited for him to return from the Melbourne Olympics in December.

Auerbach's gamble was a success, for Russell quickly became the first black superstar in the N.B.A. He averaged almost 20 rebounds per game, more than any other player in the league. The Celtics also made two other important additions to the team: 6-foot 7-inch Tom Heinsohn, a rugged, free-shooting rookie forward from Holy Cross; and Frank Ramsey, who returned from the Army in midseason. Ramsey was known as the best substitute in the league.

But even before the newcomers arrived, the well-conditioned Celtics had sprinted to the top of the division. Then, with Russell controlling the boards, they lengthened their lead and won the Eastern title by six games. In the play-offs the Celtics swept aside their old rival, Syracuse. And waiting for them in the finals were Ben Kerner's Hawks.

Kerner was one of the game's great characters— a shrewd promoter, a compulsive trader, and an impatient man with his coaches. "He changes coaches as often as he changes dirty socks," cracked a fellow owner after Kerner had dismissed his seventh coach in seven seasons.

Kerner also believed in changing players—which wasn't a bad idea since most of those he had (with the exception of his great 6-foot 9-inch forward, Bob Pettit) weren't much good anyway. Before the 1956-57 season began, Kerner really went shopping. In addition to Macauley and Hagan, he acquired guard Jack McMahon and forward Jack Coleman from Rochester. Then, in one of his finest trades, he sent another top rookie, Willie Naulls, to New York for the aging but still dangerous Slater Martin.

When the season started, Kerner turned his attention to his coaches. First he fired Red Holzman. Then he tried Martin as a player-coach. Martin didn't like the job, so Kerner looked farther down the bench and bestowed the dubious privilege on Alex Hannum, a seldom-used, 31-year-old forward. Hannum wasn't doing very much anyway, so he took the job.

Alex needed a few games to assert himself. In the meantime, the Hawks seemed more like a town meeting than a basketball team. For example, during one early game the enthusiastic Hannum was exhorting his players from the sidelines; veteran Jack Coleman was yelling some advice to Med Park; another veteran, Charlie Share, was badgering the officials about a call; and Martin was trying to move McMahon to another spot on the floor. In the midst of all this noise, referee Arnie Heft blew his whistle and walked over to the Hawks' bench. A technical foul seemed certain. "I've just got to get one thing straight," Heft said. "Which one of you guys is coaching the team today?"

"We all are," Hannum said cheerily. "This is a team effort."

"That's nice," said Heft. "But you'd better hold an election and vote who's in charge today. I can't listen to all of you."

Despite the chaotic beginning, things soon fell into place as Hannum drove, cajoled and coaxed his team toward victory. With Martin and McMahon coolly directing the team's attack and Pettit and Macauley among the league's top scorers, the surging Hawks finished with a rush to catch Minneapolis and Fort Wayne in the final week of the regular season. The race ended in a three-way tie. St. Louis was awarded first place when it won a special round-robin series. Then the Hawks captured the Western play-offs by defeating the Lakers in three straight games. Kerner and his Hawks had reached the finals at last.

The first game in Boston set the tone of what was to be an epic play-off. Pettit poured in his favorite base-line jump shots and the Hawks took a 31-21 first-quarter lead. But after three quarters, Boston caught up and moved ahead, 74-70. For the rest of the game the score seesawed back and forth.

St. Louis, anxious to win on Boston's home court, struggled to a 102-100 lead with just 20 seconds of playing time left. The sure-handed Martin was given the ball to dribble out the clock. But Cousy (as Bob Davies had done to him three years earlier) swept in like a hawk to steal the ball. He passed it to Sharman, who missed a jumper, but Heinsohn tipped the ball in with five seconds left to tie the score at 102-102 and send the game into overtime. St. Louis controlled the extra period only to see Cousy tie the score, 113-113, with a clutch 20-foot set shot in the closing seconds. A second overtime would be necessary.

Bob Pettit scores during the first game of the 1956–57 play-offs.

This time the Hawks had to fight from behind. Slowly they narrowed the Celtics' lead. With a minute left, Pettit—who led all scorers with 37 points—burst through for a lay-up over Russell's flailing hand. The game was tied again, 123-123. Cousy was fouled. But he missed the foul shot and St. Louis got the rebound. There were 54 seconds left to play.

St. Louis lacked depth and had no dependable substitutes to send into the game. On the other hand, Boston had an excellent bench. If the game went another overtime, St. Louis' chances would be slim. It was now or never for the exhausted Hawks.

Hannum instructed his team to work for a good shot. But they almost overdid it. The Hawks had had the ball for nearly the regulation 24 seconds without shooting when Jack Coleman suddenly found himself with it—and his back was turned to the basket, 15 feet away. Dumbfounded, he whirled and blindly flung the ball sidearm. As the crowd moaned in disbelief, it swished through the hoop. Boston attacked once more, but the Hawks' defense was so tight that the Celtics couldn't get off a shot. The buzzer sounded with St. Louis ahead, 125-123. "It was my specialty shot," grinned Coleman in the jubilant dressing room. "I've been practicing that one for a long time."

The second game came a day later in Boston, and now Auerbach could take advantage of his greater team depth. During the first half he kept pouring in fresh men, a tactic that eventually wore down the weary Hawks.

As it would be for a decade, the Celtics' fast break was a study in perfection. Russell would clear the boards, flip the ball to Cousy, who would dart downcourt with Sharman trailing. Then Cousy would either drive for the basket or flip the ball back to Sharman for his deadly jump shot.

Russell's shot-blocking kept St. Louis from driving down the middle of the court and the Celtics coasted to a 119-99 victory. Cousy and Ramsey scored 22 points each. More important was Heinsohn and Russell's coverage of Pettit. They limited the Hawks' star to a scant 11 points.

After a six-day rest the two teams met again in St. Louis. Just before the game there was a clash between Auerbach and Kerner, demonstrating the highly emotional atmosphere that existed during the play-offs. The trouble started when the Celtics complained that the practice balls furnished by St. Louis were "cold, wet and worn out." A few minutes later Cousy and Sharman came to the startling conclusion that Boston's basket was too low. But the referees measured both baskets and ruled that they were the required ten feet off the floor. Ben Kerner, however, was incensed by the Celtics' complaints. His face flushed with anger, he charged onto the court to confront Auerbach. One word led to another and the two men came to blows. They were separated, but the hard feelings remained.

After the two teams had settled down, the game got under way. Bob Pettit showed the benefits of his six-day rest by making 26 points and 28 rebounds. He led the Hawks to a pulsating 100-98 victory by scoring the winning basket on a 30-foot jump shot in the last 45 seconds of the game.

The loss, plus the incident with Kerner, didn't leave Auerbach in the gentlest of moods. The Celt-

Cousy passes off to Tommy Heinsohn during the second game of the play-offs.

ics reflected his boiling spirit the following day, when they blitzed St. Louis with their unstoppable fast break. Although Pettit had a great first quarter with 15 points, the lean forward quickly tired and sat out much of the second and third periods, during which the Celtics built up an 85-67 lead.

Hagan, a rookie who had matured greatly in the closing weeks of the season, and Martin gave the Celtics a scare by leading a brilliant counterattack that cut their lead to 118-117 with 1 minute and 37 seconds left. But Boston tightened its defense and went on to win, 123-118. Pettit, despite his weariness, again topped the scoring with 33 points. Cousy had one of his great outside shooting nights to finish with 31. The series was tied again, two games apiece.

The teams returned to Boston for their next game, four days later. St. Louis controlled the first half and left the court with a 60-59 lead. But the Hawks ran out of gas in the final 24 minutes. Russell dominated the boards and Pettit, who scored 33 points, got only one rebound in the last half. Sharman shot over the tiring Hawk defenders for 32 points and Boston won decisively, 124-109.

Throughout most of the sixth game in St. Louis the Hawks trailed. But, faced with elimination, they rallied in the final quarter. With only seconds remaining and the score tied, 94-94, St. Louis got the ball. Hannum instructed the Hawks to set up Pettit, who had already scored 32 points. Patiently they worked for the final shot. As the hand on the clock approached zero, Pettit sent a soft jumper toward the hoop. The ball hit the rim and spun off, but Hagan leaped up to tap it in. The buzzer sounded. St. Louis had won, 96-94. Waving their fists in triumph, the Hawks carried Hagan off the court on their shoulders. They were going back to Boston for the seventh game.

Boston Garden was a caldron of tension and noise as a capacity crowd of 13,909 screamed for the Celtics' first world championship. But Pettit's inspired play gave St. Louis a 28-26 lead at the end of the first quarter.

Hannum had aroused his club to an emotional fury, especially Martin and McMahon. Martin had experienced four titles during his years at Minneapolis and now he wanted another. The tough little Texan always played well against Cousy, for he was fast enough to keep Cooz from getting the

During the fifth game of the play-offs, Cousy dribbles down the court with St. Louis' Jack McMahon in close pursuit.

Heinsohn scores over the Hawks' Jack Coleman in the seventh game.

necessary room to maneuver. He and McMahon played Cousy and Sharman so closely that the high-scoring pair was virtually helpless, scoring on just eight of 40 shots during the entire game.

But while the St. Louis defense was occupied with Cousy and Sharman, Heinsohn took up the slack. Throwing in running hooks and off-balance jumpers from every angle, the rookie kept the Celtics in contention. At half time St. Louis led, 53-51. But the excitement was just beginning. Before the afternoon was over, the game was tied 28 times and the lead changed 38 times.

The third quarter belonged to Boston. Russell hovered about the basket like a gigantic bird, blocking shots, grabbing rebounds and intimidating the Hawks' shooters. Heinsohn continued to hit and the quarter ended with the Celtics ahead, 83-77. Auerbach seemed to be just 12 minutes away from his first championship.

But the plucky Hawks came roaring back and suddenly Boston's lead evaporated. With Hannum shouting wildly from the bench and Pettit smoothly maneuvering for his deadly jumpers, St. Louis took a 101-97 lead. The clock showed 1 minute and 40 seconds remaining when Cousy brought the Celtics back. Fouls against him gave Cousy two free throws. He made both shots, thereby narrowing St. Louis' margin to 101-99. A moment later Boston led, 102-101. Then Cousy was fouled again, and he calmly hit his shot to put the Celtics ahead by two points with just 12 seconds left to play.

Hannum, on the brink of defeat, put his faith in his best player—Pettit. As Boston fans pressed close to the court, ready to carry off the victorious Celtics, the Hawks worked the ball to their star forward. Pettit went up for his jumper and was fouled by Russell. Pettit made both of his free throws and sent the game into overtime.

Nervously clutching the crumpled program in his hand throughout the next period, Auerbach watched as the Celtics fell behind, 109-105. But

Frank Ramsey, the "super-sub," hit twice to tie the score. Then, with 15 seconds remaining, Heinsohn drove through the Hawks' defense and slammed in a lay-up. Boston led, 113-111.

The Celtics expected St. Louis to feed the ball to Pettit once more. But the Hawks fooled them. Coleman took the shot and his one-hander went in to tie the game again. Boston quickly fed the ball to Sharman. With McMahon's hand waving in his face, Bill fired as the buzzer went off. The ball rimmed the basket and fell out. A second overtime would be necessary.

The pressure was nearly unbearable as the team traded baskets. With 2 minutes and 16 seconds left, a long jump-shot by Heinsohn pushed Boston ahead, 121-120. But six seconds later the rookie fouled out of the game. Exhausted and emotionally spent, he staggered toward the dressing room until the shouts of his teammates reminded him that the game was not yet over. Slowly he turned and walked back to the bench, where he collapsed in tears and buried his face in a towel.

Martin made one of two foul shots to tie the score. Then Ramsey drove and was fouled by Macauley. Because it was his sixth personal violation Macauley had to leave the game, the fourth Hawk to foul out. Now Coach Hannum was the last big man left on the St. Louis bench. He had played in only one of the Hawks' nine previous play-off games and

After fouling out, Heinsohn collapses in tears and buries his face in a towel.

his regular-season average was a low 3.2 points per game. But he had no choice. He had to go in.

Ramsey's foul shot put Boston ahead, 122-121. Then Russell blocked another St. Louis shot and Ramsey threw in a 20-footer. The Hawks trailed by three points.

But Martin hit a free throw. St. Louis stole the ball and substitute Med Park was fouled in the act of shooting. He would get two foul shots. If he made both the score would be tied. His first shot was good. But the second hit the rim and Russell's powerful hands grasped the rebound.

With 12 seconds left, Boston led, 124-123. St. Louis could not steal the ball from Cousy, so the desperate Hannum fouled Jim Loscutoff. The muscular Boston forward hit the free throw. Then Hannum signaled for a time-out. The Hawks had the ball, but they seemed to be in an impossible position. They trailed, 125-123, and there were two seconds left to play.

Hannum would not concede defeat, however. He knew the clock would not start until someone on the court touched the inbounds pass. His plan was to throw the ball the length of the court, hit the backboard and have Pettit tap in the rebound. And it almost worked.

The balding coach's throw was perfect. The ball bounced against the backboard and into Pettit's hands. Six feet from the hoop, Bob threw a hurried shot. The crowd gasped as the ball rolled around the rim—once, twice, and out.

Bedlam broke loose. Boston had won, 125-123. The frustration was over. The Hawks had made a valiant effort, but the Celtics were champions of the world. Auerbach was tossed into the shower with his clothes on and had to spend the first night as a champion wearing a pair of faded sweat pants and an old Celtic jersey. But Red couldn't have cared less. The greatest dynasty in the history of professional sports had claimed its first title.

nine

BOB PETTIT'S VINDICATION

If ever an athlete waged a one-man crusade, it was Bob Pettit during the 1957-58 season. He could not shake the nightmare of his last futile shot against Boston in the 1957 play-offs. "We fought all year for that chance," he reminded himself, "and then I had to blow the big shot at the end."

Pettit was a proud man and he knew that until he had led St. Louis to a championship, hopefully over Boston, he would not be able to shed the pain of that missed shot. When the new season began he took his frustration out on the opposition in a cascade of baskets and rebounds. Then, just as he was leading the league in scoring and the Hawks were running away with the Western division race, Pettit broke a bone below the thumb on his left hand. Furious at his bad luck, he insisted on playing despite a cumbersome cast.

Even though they were handicapped by their star player's injury, the Hawks easily won the Western division title, and Pettit managed to finish third in scoring with a 24.6 average. Then the Hawks crushed the Pistons, four games to one, in the semifinals of the play-offs. They had reached the finals again. And, just as before, Boston was waiting for them.

St. Louis had the same starters it had used in 1957. Pettit and Cliff Hagan were the forwards. Easy Ed Macauley and Charlie Share split the center's duties and Slater Martin and Don McMahon were the guards. The stage was set for one of the most eagerly anticipated rematches in sports.

The Hawks were grim as they flew to Boston to begin their crusade. Share typified the Hawks' determination. The 6-foot 11-inch center had vowed to play despite the fact that his jaw was broken and had been wired closed. "It's very sore," Share said, "but I'm just going to have to wait until after the series before anything else can be done. It's a soup and ice-cream diet for me. We all hope it's steak and champagne when this is over."

The Hawks would meet a Celtic club little changed from the year before, except that they were stronger and more experienced. The incomparable Bill Russell was the center, Bob Cousy and Bill Sharman the guards, Tom Heinsohn a forward, and Frank Ramsey was the vital "sixth man." The only new starter was rookie Lou Tsioropoulos, who had replaced the injured "Jungle Jim" Loscutoff.

The opening game was rugged, fast-moving and exciting. Although the Celtics trailed, 59-53, at half time, they fought back into an 83-80 lead as the fourth quarter began. St. Louis moved ahead, but with 2 minutes and 30 seconds left to play, Boston narrowed the lead to 101-100. Then Pettit got a free throw and tipped in a rebound to widen the gap to 104-100. Boston could manage only two free throws in the final minutes and the Hawks won the opener, 104-102. Pettit had scored 30 points and Hagan, held to 10 points in the first half, wound up with 33. Cousy had scored 27 and Sharman 25 for the Celtics.

The Hawks' dressing room was an effervescent scene. But Martin, the wise campaigner, urged caution: "We won the first one here last year and still lost the series."

Down the hall, Auerbach grimly called St. Louis "a much better team than last year" and predicted a tougher fight, if that was possible.

As usual, the Celtics came battling back. Scoring on over 50 percent of their shots from the floor, they built up a 17-point lead early in the second

Tommy Heinsohn lands on the back of the Hawks' Chuck Share after a scoring attempt in the first game.

The Hawks and the Celtics battle for a loose ball during the second game.

period, then coasted to a 136-112 victory. But once again the Celtics failed to stop Hagan, who chalked up 37 points. However, Russell out-rebounded Pettit, 27-7.

Back in St. Louis for the third game, the teams fought to a 49-49 deadlock at half time. Then came the turning point of the series. As Pettit drove for the basket, Russell leapt high above the rim to block the shot. But as he came down, the Celtics' great center landed heavily on his right ankle and collapsed in a heap on the floor. He had suffered a severe sprain and, as a result, the Celtics were in serious trouble.

Now that Russell was out of the game, the Boston defense was vulnerable to the driving shots of Pettit and Hagan (who finished with 32 and 18 points respectively). The Hawks roared to an 80-65 lead.

Trying for a lay-up in the third game, little Slater Martin is dwarfed by Bill Russell.

Russell returned for a moment, but his ankle could not support him and he limped off the floor to watch the remainder of the game from the bench.

In the huddle between quarters, Auerbach gave his team a tongue-lashing. Now, he said, they would have to prove that they were good enough to win without Russell. The Celtics, moved by their coach's talk, began the fourth period with renewed determination. Ramsey and Sharman poured in shots and Boston swept through the St. Louis defense, finally narrowing the margin to 106-104. A moment later St. Louis increased its lead to 108-104. The clock showed a minute of playing time.

Ramsey brought the Celtics back with two free throws, but Martin widened the gap to 110-106. Boston needed a basket in a hurry. And Sam Jones, a rookie who had played very little during the regular season, came through with a 30-foot one-hander that swished through the net for two points. Just 25 seconds remained.

St. Louis moved downcourt and, for no apparent reason, neglected to use up the allotted 24 seconds before shooting. Instead the Hawks fired quickly and missed. Boston took the rebound with 17 seconds left.

The Celtics worked hurriedly, looking for a three-point play. Then they committed an error in the clutch—something unusual for the Celtics.

Sharman's pass was high and glanced off Sam Jones' hands. Macauley dashed in to pick it up. Just before the buzzer, Cousy fouled Martin, whose free throw brought the final score to 111-108. The Celtics now trailed two games to one.

Although there was a gloomy air in the Boston locker room, there was no talk of defeat. The Celtics were too proud for that. The players even spoke of Russell making a speedy recovery, but the injured center was in agony. "It's so tender I can't even bandage the ankle," he admitted.

In another corner of the room sat Tommie Heinsohn. He had scored only 11 points and he was steaming. "I can't remember having two frightful games back to back as I've had in this series," he sputtered. "But I'm going to make up for it."

Aware that his team needed help, Auerbach concocted some surprises for St. Louis in the fourth game. Since neither of his aging reserve-centers, Arnie Risen and Jack Nichols, had the strength or speed to handle Pettit, Share and Macauley, Auerbach told the fired-up Heinsohn to guard Pettit.

However, the biggest surprise involved Cousy. In the second quarter, the 6-foot 1-inch guard moved into the pivot position. With Russell on the bench, Auerbach had decided that he might as well take advantage of Cousy's 3-inch height advantage over Martin.

The strategy worked beautifully. Even though he played with a pulled tendon in his leg, Cousy still tossed in hook shots with either hand, slipped outside for long set shots and scored 16 points in the quarter. Boston led, 57-51, at the half.

Auerbach continued to befuddle St. Louis in the last two quarters. He shifted players constantly— moving Cousy in and out of the pivot—and often instructed his club to slow the game to a walk in order to throw the Hawks off stride.

Disorganized and baffled, the Hawks lost, 109-98. Cousy, playing one of the greatest games of his career, finished with 24 points, 10 assists and 13 rebounds. Heinsohn, usually an offense-oriented player, had guarded Pettit so effectively that the Hawks' star had scored only 12 points.

When the teams moved to Boston for the fifth game, Hawk coach Alex Hannum had a surprise of his own. As soon as Cousy would shift into the pivot, as he had so successfully in the previous contest, Slater Martin would slip in front of him, instead of covering him from behind. As a result, Cousy was unable to get the ball very often and the Celtics' offense was bottled up.

Forced to shoot from outside and handicapped by Russell's absence, the Celtics made only 24 percent of their shots from the field. In contrast, Pettit dominated Heinsohn around the basket and

Pettit (9) snags a rebound from Heinsohn (15) during the fifth game.

Martin scored steadily against Cousy. St. Louis led at half time, 58-43.

The third quarter ended with the Hawks still in front, 84-70. It was clear that Boston would have to do something drastic to get back into the game. So Auerbach sent the Celtics into a "full-court press," with three guards and two short forwards.

St. Louis was caught off balance and began to lose the ball. Only a minute of playing time remained when the Celtics cut the margin to 101-94.

Cousey banked in a one-hander to bring the score to 101-96. The Hawks tried to set Pettit up for an inside shot, but the pass was batted away and Cousy emerged from the scramble of arms and legs dribbling the ball. Quickly, Cooz passed to Ramsey under the basket and the "super-sub" scored to reduce the margin to 101-98. The sellout crowd in Boston Garden was on its feet screaming.

Moments later, the Celtics took possession of the ball again. Cousy's hurried one-hander hit the rim, but Ramsey leaped up once more to tap it in.

The Hawks' Jack McMahon drives in for a shot during the fifth game.

Boston trailed by one point with 16 seconds to go.

Martin frantically dribbled upcourt as the Celtics swarmed around him. For a moment it seemed that he would not get the ball over midcourt in the required 10 seconds. Martin crossed the center line just as the referee's count reached ten. The Celtics protested that Martin had not made it in time, but the referee disagreed. St. Louis still had the ball.

Cousy fouled Martin just before the buzzer sounded, giving St. Louis a free throw. The shot was good and a moment later the game was over. St. Louis had won, 102-100. Pettit was one victory away from his vindication.

From the moment the sixth game started, before a cheering, stomping crowd of 10,218 in St. Louis, it was clear that Pettit had not forgotten his mission to erase the memory of the previous season's defeat. He scored the first basket of the game on a 20-foot jump shot. By half time he had 19 points and St. Louis led, 57-52.

In the third quarter, after Pettit had scored six points in a row to push the Hawks ahead by 10, Cousy's brilliant ball handling cut St. Louis' lead to 83-77. Then, at the start of the final quarter, the Celtics threw their offense into high gear. Tsioropoulos hit two field goals and Ramsey and Sharman one each. Sharman added a foul shot and Boston led, 86-84. The Hawks seemed unable to find the basket and were in danger of having the play-offs return to Boston for the seventh game.

Pettit was painfully aware of this and was determined to avoid another summer of unhappiness. He had tasted defeat too often throughout his career with the Hawks. Suddenly he was a one-man team and the Celtics could not stop him.

"Pettit was a madman," Sharman recalled later. "He was going up in the keyhole so high that Arnie Risen [6-feet 9-inches] couldn't stay with him. In every huddle we asked each other: 'How can we stop Pettit?' We tried sagging on him and then two-manning him when he made his move. We tried to stop the Hawks from passing to him. We even tried using Heinsohn to guard him face-to-face when he didn't have the ball. We might as well have tried to bribe the guy to take it easy. He just killed us."

Weaving, wheeling, feinting and forcing his way relentlessly toward the basket, Pettit awed the Celtics and drew thunderous applause from the crowd.

Playing for the first time since the third game and limping with a cast around his injured ankle, Russell tried vainly to contain Pettit. But nothing could stop the Hawks' great forward. Pettit's name echoed over the public-address system as shot after shot tore through the net: a one-hander, a three-point play, a twisting jumper, a driving lay-up. The Celtics were fouling Pettit almost every time he got the ball, but it was futile. With just 2 minutes and 10 seconds remaining in the game, St. Louis led, 105-100.

But the Celtics were far from finished. Cousy seemed to be all over the court. With 25 seconds left, he hit two foul shots and a long set-shot. The Hawks led by only one point now. Win Wilfong of St. Louis connected on a foul shot. But Heinsohn also scored from the foul line to keep Boston within striking distance. The tension mounted on each team until it was practically unbearable.

"Get it to Pettit! Get it to Pettit!" Hannum shouted over the deafening noise. The Hawks' star took the ball and drove on Russell, who strained to leap on his throbbing leg. But Pettit jumped and arched the ball over Russell's clawing hand into the basket. The score was 108-105.

The Celtics came back once more. Heinsohn bulled his way toward the basket and was fouled in the act of shooting. There were 16 seconds left. Heinsohn hit both shots.

The Hawks led, 108-107, as Martin dribbled through the Celtics' press. With the entire Boston defense converging on Pettit, Martin had to try a set shot. The ball was off target and the spectators groaned. But Pettit, a man possessed, jumped up to

tap in the rebound. And that decided the game.

Although Boston scored another basket, Martin dribbled out the final seconds and St. Louis won, 110-109. Suddenly the court was covered with happy fans, who hoisted Pettit to their shoulders and carried him toward the locker room.

Bob Pettit had swept away the memory of 1957 with a flood of points and had finished the game with a play-off record of 50 (18 out of St. Louis' last 21). The Hawks were champions of the world.

For Boston there was no shame, however. The Celtics had played bravely without Russell, displaying the ability that would enable them to win the N.B.A. title for the next eight seasons in a row. But, years later, Auerbach would still needle Heinsohn: "We would have won in 1958, too, if you had held Pettit to 48 points."

After leading the Hawks to a 110–109 victory, Pettit is surrounded by happy fans.

ten

WILT HITS 100

There are hundreds of men who stand over seven feet tall. But there is only one Wilt Chamberlain. When he joined the Philadelphia Warriors in 1959, he quickly made the N.B.A. record book seem like his personal publication. That season he led the league in scoring and rebounding. The next year he led in scoring, rebounding and shooting percentage. And though the Warriors, a last-place team before Wilt arrived, could not overtake the Boston Celtics in the Eastern division, Chamberlain transformed them into a winning club.

Then, in 1961-62, "The Dipper," as Wilt called himself, enjoyed the greatest offensive season in the history of pro basketball. He scored 50 points or more in 46 of the team's 80 games and finished the regular season with an incredible average of 50.4 points per game.

In Los Angeles, on December 8, 1961, Chamberlain broke the league scoring record with 78 points in a triple-overtime contest. A month later he scored 73 points against Chicago to break Elgin Baylor's mark of 71 for a regulation game.

"My record isn't going to stand long," Baylor had said before Chamberlain's historic feat. "Some day soon somebody is going to score a hundred points in a game. There's no ceiling except time on how many points a man can score."

The night Wilt scored 78, Frank McGuire, the Warriors' coach, warned: "Some day soon Chamberlain is going to score a hundred. He'll do it even if five men guard him."

Then, on March 2, 1962, the Warriors traveled to Hershey, Pennsylvania, to meet the last-place New York Knicks on a neutral court. No one expected very much to happen. Only five games remained in the regular season. The Warriors had second place safety tucked away and were just waiting for the play-offs to start. In fact, the New York papers didn't even send reporters to cover the game.

When Wilt came out on the court he received a big cheer from the crowd. At first, however, Chamberlain seemed a bit lethargic. Then he began to grin, for someone was playing his record over the public-address system. A month before, "The Dipper" had made his first—and only—attempt at a singing career when he cut a rock 'n' roll record called "By the River." It wasn't a memorable piece of music, but Wilt enjoyed it. When he heard it that night, he seemed to loosen up. And throughout the warm-ups, he was humming and laughing.

But when the game started Chamberlain gave the Knicks nothing to laugh about, especially husky, 6-foot 10-inch Darrall Imhoff, who was substituting for the injured starting center. Chamberlain began scoring at a furious pace. Before the Knicks knew what had hit them, Wilt had collected 13 points, including seven successful foul shots in a row. Philadelphia led, 19-3.

Wilt's foul shooting made it clear that it was no ordinary night. For, despite his incredible scoring ability, Chamberlain was practically unchallenged as the worst foul shooter in the league. But that night he wasn't missing from the foul line. "I went into the game relaxed," he said later. "And when I made those ten straight foul shots [he hit three more before he missed], I thought I could get some kind of foul-shooting record. I wasn't thinking about a game record then."

The first quarter ended with Philadelphia ahead, 42-26. Wilt had hit seven of 14 shots from the field and already had 23 points. By now, a game record was on everyone's mind.

During the next quarter, Chamberlain banked in jump shots over Imhoff's straining hand, bulled through the defense to stuff rebounds with his frightening dunk shot, slipped in his underhand "dipper" and even raced down the floor to follow up shots after a fast break. "He was so strong," Imhoff recalled later, "that he was picking us up and stuffing us through the hoop along with the ball. We collapsed three men around him and it didn't do any good. And I don't think I've ever seen him getting down the floor so fast. I couldn't keep up with him."

Despite Chamberlain's devastating performance, New York didn't quit. Imhoff and Willie Naulls battled the muscular center desperately and the Knicks cut the Warriors' lead slightly. But by half time they were still behind, 79-68. Wilt had sunk seven of 12 shots in the second quarter and had a total of 41 points.

In the Philadelphia locker room, no one spoke of a record. But Chamberlain's teammates knew that if he could continue his pace he had a shot at it. By now Imhoff was on the bench with foul trouble. While he was out of the game the Knicks had to use slim, 6-foot 7-inch Cleveland Buckner against Chamberlain. It is unlikely that anyone could have stopped Wilt that night and Buckner clearly didn't have a chance.

In the third quarter Wilt hit 10 of 16 shots. His dunks seemed to explode through the basket and his fallaway jumpers rattled off the backboard into the hoop. Going into the final 12 minutes, the Warriors led, 125-106. Wilt had 69 points, just four short of his own record for a regulation game.

Now the Warriors were working seriously at feeding the ball to Chamberlain. Wilt spun a "dipper" under Buckner's arm. The ball curled into the basket. Wilt banked in a jump shot. With 10 minutes and 10 seconds remaining he slammed in a rebound. He had 75 points—a new record.

Imhoff returned but fouled out, making it even harder for the Knicks to contain Wilt. There were 7 minutes and 51 seconds left to play when Chamberlain took a pass from Guy Rodgers and swished in a one-hander from the foul line for his 79th point. The crowd's applause was deafening, for no one had ever scored more in a professional game.

As the clock ticked away, the fans began to chant: "GIVE IT TO WILT. GIVE IT TO WILT." His teammates responded. With a little over 5 minutes to go, Al Attles, who hadn't missed a shot in eight attempts, passed up an easy basket to lob the ball to Wilt. The giant center leaped high above the hoop and rammed the ball through. He had 89 points.

At that point the Knicks called a time-out. They had to do something to avoid the embarrassment of being the first pro team to allow a player to score 100 points in a single game. Coach Ed Donovan ordered his club to stall as long as the 24-second clock would allow. The Knicks also started fouling the other Warriors in order to keep Wilt from getting the ball. For the next two minutes, while his teammates made free throws, Chamberlain was scoreless. His chance for 100 points seemed to be slipping away.

To counter New York's tactics, Coach Frank McGuire sent three Philadelphia substitutes, York Larese, Joe Ruklick and Ted Luckenbill, into the game with orders to foul the Knicks as soon as New York had the ball. This ruined the Knicks' stall and got the ball for Philadelphia. Then the Warriors would pass to Wilt so quickly that New York wouldn't have a chance to foul them. Chamberlain began to score again.

The frantic Knicks "collapsed" their defense around Wilt, continually fouling him. But Wilt still wasn't missing his free throws Three shots from the foul line and a long jump shot gave him 94 points. The crowd was on its feet screaming.

Rodgers dribbled the ball over midcourt, slipped away from his defender and whipped a pass to Wilt. The ball bounced out of Chamberlain's hands, but the big man recovered it, twisted around and flipped in another jump shot for his 96th point.

Then the Knicks tried to freeze the ball, but it got loose. Larese picked it up and moved into the forecourt. When Wilt had positioned himself near the basket, Larese lofted a high pass above the heads of Buckner, Naulls and the other Knicks. Chamberlain reached over them, grabbed the ball and dunked it. The building rocked with noise. The Warriors on the bench were standing and shouting. Wilt had 98 points with 1 minute and 19 seconds to go.

The Knicks tried to pass the ball in bounds, but Chamberlain slipped in to intercept it. He fired a hurried one-hander. It hit the rim and bounced off.

New York brought the ball down the court and missed a shot. Philadelphia took the rebound and Ruklick fed the ball to Chamberlain in the pivot. Wilt missed, grabbed the rebound and missed again. Luckenbill outfought the Knicks for the ball and passed it to Ruklick. The clock kept running.

Ruklick saw Wilt near the basket and tossed a high pass above the rim. In one sweeping motion, Chamberlain rose up, clamped both hands on the ball and stuffed it through the basket. He had scored 100 points.

Although there were still 46 seconds left to play, over 200 fans rushed onto the court. They mobbed

Wilt sinks his 100th point.

Fans and teammates congratulate Wilt after his historic feat.

Wilt, slapping his back and shaking his hand. Even the Knicks came off the bench to congratulate him.

The buzzer sounded with Philadelphia ahead, 169-147. Wilt had scored 31 points in the final quarter. He had also finished with 25 rebounds and 36 field goals in 63 attempts. Even more amazing was the fact that he had hit 28 of 32 foul shots.

Moments later, in the dressing room, Wilt was engulfed by his happy teammates. "Honestly," he kept repeating, "I never thought I could do it. Never in my life. It's really something. Like nothing that ever happened to me before. I sure do feel different. Triple figures. Wow!"

Then he became serious: "It was just as big an effort for the team. It wouldn't even have been close to possible without them. They wanted me to get it as much as I did."

The Warriors' next game was in Madison Square Garden, so when Wilt left Hershey that night, he drove to his apartment in New York City. But he was too excited to sleep. "I was too happy to think about being tired," he said later. "I didn't get to bed until about 8 A.M. It was an amazing thing, scoring a hundred points. But I just hope nobody ever asks me when I'm going to score a hundred and twenty—because I never will."

While Wilt was driving to New York, young Darrall Imhoff, who had fouled out trying to guard him, sat alone with his thoughts at a bar in Hershey. Finally, a drunk approached him and began to mumble about nightmares. Imhoff looked up and shook his head. "I can't have a nightmare tonight," he said sadly. "I've just lived through one."

eleven

DOUBLE-BARRELED
CHALLENGE

When George Mikan retired in 1954, the Minneapolis Lakers' dynasty came to an end. One by one, the old pros either quit or were traded. Soon the team was sagging both on the court and at the box office. In 1957-58, while playing its home games in near privacy, Minneapolis fell to last place with a record of 19 wins and 53 losses.

Fortunately, their dismal finish brought the Lakers first choice in the college draft. And they chose Elgin Baylor, a 6-foot 5-inch, 225-pound forward from the University of Seattle. It was around Baylor that the Lakers began to rebuild.

For two seasons, however, Baylor *was* the Lakers. Although he was short for a pro forward, he had great power and magnificent moves. Even his opponents marveled at his unbelievable body control. Baylor seemed to hang for seconds at the top of his jump, making midair fakes and tossing off-balance shots into the basket. He could shoot, rebound, set up plays and guard any forward in the league. Many called him the best all-round player in the game.

Baylor became an instant star and during the 1958-59 season he averaged 24.9 points per game, while singlehandedly carrying his patchwork club to second place during the regular season and then to victory in the Western division play-offs. The Boston Celtics slaughtered hapless Minneapolis in the finals, but the four straight defeats did not diminish the luster of Baylor's rookie season.

The following year the Lakers went into a slump, winning only 25 and losing 50, and were quickly eliminated in the play-offs. Baylor averaged 29.6, but his heroics were not enough to attract the disinterested Minneapolis fans. So, at the end of the season, the franchise was moved to Los Angeles.

Although Baylor was obviously one of basketball's great players, the Lakers were not a respectable ball club until Jerry West arrived at the start of the first season in their new home. The All-American from West Virginia was the Lakers' number-one draft choice. A fast, clutch-shooting 6-foot 3-

inch guard, Jerry took some of the offensive pressure off Baylor and quickly became a superstar in his own right.

West and Baylor were an immediate hit with Los Angeles fans. That first season West averaged 17.6 points per game and Baylor 34.8. The Lakers rose to second place and made their way to the seventh game of the Western Division play-offs before losing to St. Louis.

Both West and the Lakers came of age in the 1961-62 season. With a year of experience under his belt, Jerry was a polished, confident leader. He averaged 30.8 points a game and even pushed Bob Cousy off the All-N.B.A. team. Baylor averaged 38.2, second only to Wilt Chamberlain.

But West and Baylor were not the entire Los Angeles team. Coach Fred Schaus had a solid starting five. Frank Selvy, a steady, accurate guard, teamed with West in the backcourt and averaged 14.7. Rudy LaRusso, a rugged defender and consistent rebounder, played opposite Baylor at forward, averaging 17.1. And 6-foot 8-inch Jim Krebs, a competent pivot man, held down the center spot.

The Lakers were a youthful team and their energy carried them all the way to the top of the Western division, where they finished 11 games ahead of the aging Hawks. Then Los Angeles crushed Detroit in the play-offs. The brash upstarts from the West were ready to challenge the Boston Celtics for the N.B.A. championship.

After losing their title to St. Louis in 1958, the Celtics had made a brilliant comeback. They had beaten Minneapolis in 1959 and knocked off the Hawks in both the 1960 and 1961 finals. Now, in 1962, they were at the peak of their power.

Boston had opened the season by winning 23 of its first 26 games and then coasted home, 11 games ahead of Philadelphia. By this time, Cousy was 33 years old, an advanced age for a basketball player, yet he still ran the club with his incomparable passing. Bill Sharman had retired, but his guard position was shared by the two Jones boys—Sam and K.C. They were not related and neither were their skills. But both were great players. Sam was a brilliant jump-shooter and K.C. was the toughest defensive guard in the league.

In the front court the Celtics were even more powerful. Bill Russell, at center, was acclaimed as the finest defensive player in basketball history and had made a runaway of the M.V.P. balloting that year. The forwards were the veteran Tom Heinsohn and an excellent defensive player named Tom Sanders. On the bench Auerbach had Frank Ramsey, known as "Mr. Clutch," and "Jungle Jim" Loscutoff, the N.B.A.'s most feared muscleman.

In spite of its formidable line-up, Boston had almost lost the Eastern division play-offs to Philadelphia. Wilt Chamberlain had carried the Warriors through seven spine-tingling games before the Celtics rallied to win, 109-107.

When it was over, a nervous, sweat-drenched Auerbach had wiped his forehead and mumbled weakly: "That was absolutely the toughest play-off series we've ever been through."

It wasn't the toughest for long, however.

The Celtics entered the first game of the championship finals weary and battle-scarred after struggling through five games in the last eight days. The frisky Lakers, on the other hand, arrived in Boston rested and ready.

But the Celtics showed no signs of exhaustion. Instead, the Lakers were the ones to run out of gas. K. C. Jones seemed to clamp himself to West and every time Jerry moved the ball into the forecourt, K.C. would be staring him in the eye. When West drove for the basket Jones would stay in front of him, forcing him to veer off and to take bad shots. Even when West didn't have the ball, K.C. stayed close, using his powerful body to bump the Lakers' star off-stride. As a result, West often missed his shots and finished with only 21 points. Baylor managed to score 35, but Boston still won easily, 122-108. The Celtics appeared headed for a four-game sweep.

But Los Angeles would concede nothing and went into the second game determined to make their challenge felt. West, angered by his relatively poor performance in the first game, darted behind screens set up by his stationary teammates and tossed in arching jump shots. He scored the Lakers' first 11 points and continued his barrage as Los Angeles galloped to a 90-66 lead in the third quarter.

Then Auerbach sent Ramsey into the game. The "super-sub" promptly led the Celtics on another of their blitzing comebacks. At the end of the quarter, the Lakers staggered into the huddle with a slender 102-98 lead.

Rudy LaRusso (35), Frank Ramsey (23) and Bill Russell go after a loose ball.

Boston continued its relentless pressure in the fourth quarter. With 5 minutes and 50 seconds remaining, the Celtics finally moved ahead, 112-111. Everyone in Boston Garden expected Los Angeles to disintegrate, as most Boston opponents did when the stampede was on.

This was the crucial moment of the series and, to the surprise of Celtic fans, the Lakers didn't fold. West dribbled past K.C. Jones and dipped his shoulders as though he was going to try a jumper. Russell sprang up to block the shot. But Jerry held the ball, waiting until Russell had reached the top of his leap and was coming down. Then he fired the ball over Russell's finger tips into the basket. Los Angeles led, 113-112.

West followed with another field goal and after that all the Lakers caught fire, coasting to a 129-122 victory. The Los Angeles players were grinning confidently as they walked to their locker room. They no longer held the Celtics in awe—and Boston knew it.

In the third game, before a record crowd of 15,180 at the Los Angeles Sports Arena, West and Baylor went on another scoring spree. With seven minutes left, Los Angeles led, 103-91. Then, with only 58 seconds remaining, Boston moved ahead, 115-111. But Jerry West exploded once more. He hit a long jump shot and followed with two free

After stealing the ball from the startled Cousy, Jerry West sinks the winning basket in the third game.

throws to tie the game, 115-115, with 5 seconds left to play.

Boston called a time-out. The Arena was a bedlam of noise. Auerbach set up a play and the Lakers knew they had to stop it in order to send the game into overtime. Sam Jones passed toward Cousy. But West, sensing the play, suddenly darted in front of

Cooz and intercepted the ball in midflight. He dribbled three times and banked in a lay-up as the buzzer sounded. The Lakers had won, 117-115.

Baylor had scored 39 points. And West, who finished with 36, had scored four crucial points in the last five seconds. He was crying from joy and emotional fatigue as his teammates carried him off the court on their shoulders.

Under the other basket, Cousy walked off alone, tears burning in his eyes. The Celtics could not believe the amazing turn of events. To top off the evening, they returned to their dressing room to find the door locked.

In the fourth game, all Boston's pent-up fury came crashing down on the young challengers. Although Baylor scored 38 points and West 26, the Lakers were never really in contention. Russell humiliated Krebs around the basket and fired in 21 points. Cousy picked apart the Los Angeles defense and the Celtics breezed to a 115-103 victory. "When Russ goes to the basket," Cousy exclaimed after the game, "there isn't anyone on the Laker club who can stop him."

The series was tied, two games apiece, and the pendulum had swung back toward the Celtics.

On the plane to Boston, Baylor sat alone with his thoughts. Usually he was so talkative that his teammates had dubbed him "Motormouth." But now he

Cousy fires a jump shot in the fourth game.

was quiet. Los Angeles needed a lift and he knew that it was up to him to supply it. For some reason, the Celtics always seemed to make Baylor's adrenalin flow. In five games that season he had scored over 50 points against them. But even Baylor was to be surprised at his performance in the fifth game of the series.

From the start it seemed that he just couldn't miss. He finished with 61 points, a new play-off record. The final score was Los Angeles 126, Boston 121. In an amazing display of accuracy, Baylor had hit 22 of 40 shots from the floor and 17 of 18 from the free-throw line. "That was the most magnificent individual effort I've ever seen in basketball," shouted the jubilant Schaus. "We'll win it now. We've got them back home."

Over 14,000 fans jammed the Sports Arena hoping to see the Celtics dethroned in the sixth game. And it seemed they would get their wish, for West and Baylor almost blew Boston off the court in the first half. Jerry scored 23 points and Elgin 21, driving the Lakers to a 65-57 lead.

Boston was on the brink of defeat, but not of despair. When they emerged for the last half, their faces were grim and determined. Sam Jones maneuvered into the corner, took a quick pass from Cousy and hit a set shot. Heinsohn made a free throw. A moment later he drilled in a two-handed jumper

Jerry West and K. C. Jones (25) fight for the ball in the crucial sixth game.

from 20 feet out and Cousy drove through for a pair of baskets. Suddenly the Boston blitz was on. Within five minutes the Celtics outscored the Lakers, 17-4, and proceeded to roll to a 119-105 victory.

Baylor and West each had 34 points, but Sam Jones topped that by scoring 35. Russell scored 19 and grabbed 24 rebounds. "This is the kind of club that meets the big challenge," Cousy said proudly in the locker room. "When we have our backs to the wall, when all seems lost, we come through." The Celtics were going back to Boston for the seventh game.

Basketball fever swept New England. Boston Garden was packed with 13,909 fans, and over 10,000 more were turned away. In the first half the intense pressure caused both teams to be over-anxious. Only Ramsey, having come off the bench once more, was hitting for Boston. He drilled in 17 points and Russell dominated the backboards. Baylor scored 22, but the Celtics led at half time, 53-47.

When the last half began, Sam Jones, who had scored only two points so far, started to find the mark. It was just in time, for Jerry West had also found the range. By the end of the third quarter, the score was tied, 75-75.

The fourth quarter was a bubbling caldron of tension and excitement. West and Baylor carried the entire Los Angeles attack and the other Lakers rarely shot. Selvy worked doggedly, feeding the

The Celtics' Frank Ramsey tries to prevent LaRusso from shooting in the final game.

ball to the superstars. Krebs and LaRusso reserved most of their energy for fighting Russell under the boards.

But Russell was too much for them—or anyone. His hands and arms were everywhere, sweeping the ball off the backboards, stuffing in rebounds and slamming shots back in the faces of West and Baylor. Sam Jones kept hitting and the Celtics moved ahead, 100-96.

The double-barreled attack by West and Baylor

had already added up to 74 points, but the Lakers were running out of time. Finally, Selvy grabbed a rebound and dribbled the length of the court to sink a driving lay-up for his first field goal of the game. But Boston still led, 100-98, and there were just 40 seconds to go.

Auerbach signaled wildly to the Celtics, imploring them to work for a good shot. Then the incomparable Cousy made a mistake. He was so intent on setting up a perfect shot that he stared straight at Sam Jones before passing the ball to him. West read Cousy's "telegraph" message and cut in front of Jones to intercept. Jerry dribbled downcourt ahead of the field. He rose towards the basket, shot the ball—and missed! But the hustling Selvy had followed the play and he tapped in the rebound. The crowd moaned. The score was tied, 100-100. Eighteen seconds remained in the game.

Boston maneuvered the ball to Ramsey, but his hook shot was no good. Los Angeles grabbed the rebound and called a time-out. There were 7 seconds left. The Celtics' dynasty would topple if Los Angeles scored.

Now Coach Schaus had to make an all-important decision. There would be time for only one more shot, but who would make it? Either Baylor or West would be a likely choice, but Schaus surprised the Lakers by selecting Selvy. He reasoned that Boston would concentrate its entire defense on West and Baylor and leave Selvy uncovered.

After taking the in-bounds pass, Selvy dribbled quickly up the left side of the court. Fifteen feet from the basket he stopped and lofted a soft jumper. Baylor rose up under the boards and his hand hovered at the rim of the basket as the ball hit. But he thought the shot was going in, so he pulled his hand back. The ball rolled off. Russell soared over Baylor, seized the ball with both hands and hugged it to his body as the buzzer sounded. The game was in overtime.

Russell, totally exhausted, sank to the floor, still holding the ball. He remained there motionless for 30 seconds. Then he rose slowly and walked to a rickety chair beside the Celtics' bench. As Auerbach and the rest of the team huddled about Russell, the trainer poured a pitcher of ice water on the back of his neck. Bill took a deep breath and stood up. As he walked to midcourt to begin the overtime the Boston Garden shook with cheers.

The Celtics missed their first shot. Then Ramsey fouled Baylor and had to leave the game because it was his sixth personal violation. Heinsohn, Loscutoff and Sanders had already fouled out trying to stop Baylor. As a result, Auerbach faced a desperate situation. The coach turned and nodded toward Gene Guarilia, an obscure substitute who had

Elgin Baylor (22) shoots despite Russell's defensive stance.

played infrequently during the regular season. Guarilia would have to guard the Lakers' great forward.

Baylor hit both of his foul shots and Los Angeles led, 102-100. The Celtics' next shot missed, but Guarilia outjumped Baylor for the rebound and passed to Russell, who dunked. The score was tied again, 102-102.

The Lakers fed the ball to Baylor, who tried to maneuver against Guarilia. But Elgin was tired and

Guarilia would not give ground. Finally Baylor fired an off-balance jumper which missed. Russell grabbed the rebound and whipped it to K.C., who passed to Sam Jones. Sam's lay-up was good and he was fouled in the process. After he hit his foul shot, the Celtics led, 105-102.

At this point the Laker bench was standing, begging Baylor to score. But Elgin's shot went astray and the Celtics took the rebound. Russell hit one of two foul shots to increase the margin to 106-102.

The frantic Lakers drove toward the basket and there was a wild scramble. Whistles blew. The referee pointed at Baylor. It was Elgin's sixth personal foul and he was out of the game. Now Los Angeles' defeat seemed certain.

Baylor had scored 41 points. As he walked sadly off the court, the normally partisan Boston fans stood and cheered. The applause was thunderous. Even the Celtic players came over to shake his hand.

With a little over a minute left Boston led, 110-103. Just before the end of the game, Auerbach started to prepare himself for a trip into the victory shower. Off came his jacket, then his cuff links. The crowd screamed with delight and counted the seconds. Auerbach was pulling off his tie when the buzzer sounded. The Celtics had won, 110-107. The dynasty had survived the challenge.

While pandemonium reigned outside, the Lakers'

locker room was silent. The double-barreled up-starts had come within an inch of dethroning the Celtics. Baylor had averaged a record 40.6 points for the seven games and West 31.1, yet the Lakers had still lost.

Selvy sat alone, his eyes fixed on his bare toes. "I missed the big one," he mumbled almost inaudibly. "I can't tell you what I felt. I just kept saying to myself, 'I missed it. I missed it. It was there for me and I missed it. All that work wasted.'"

The joy in the Boston clubhouse was tempered by fatigue. Sam Jones had scored 27 points and Ramsey 23. The victory, however, belonged to Russell. He had tied his own play-off record with 40 rebounds. He had scored 30 points and played all 53 minutes. But his ordeal had left him emotionally spent. The moment he reached the locker room he became sick. Then he began to cry.

At last Russell regained his composure. While the Celtics celebrated by pushing Auerbach in the shower and dousing each other with champagne, reporters clustered around the big center. Russell smoothed his goatee and thought aloud about the game. "This one meant more to me than any other," he smiled. "Those Lakers give me the feeling things aren't going to be the same next year."

Russell was a brilliant basketball player, but he wasn't very good at making predictions: the Celtics were world champions for the next four years.

(Above) Cousy drives past the Lakers' Frank Selvy. (Below) After stepping out of his victory shower, Auerbach talks to reporters.

twelve

WILT FINALLY WINS

No individual ever dominated a sport the way Wilt Chamberlain ruled pro basketball during his first seven years in the N.B.A. But, despite Wilt's triumphs, there was something missing. He had rewritten the record book, but he had never played on a championship team. Every season that Chamberlain had led the league in scoring, Bill Russell and the Boston Celtics had emerged as the champions of the N.B.A.

Twice the Warriors had met the Celtics in the Eastern division finals. And both time the Celtics had won. In 1963-64, Wilt got another whiff of the title when the Warriors moved to San Francisco, where they won the Western division play-offs. But again Boston was waiting for them in the championship finals, and the outcome was the same as before.

The Warriors collapsed completely in the 1964-65 season and stunned the basketball world by trading Chamberlain to the Philadelphia 76ers. Now he was back in the East—with Russell and the Celtics. At the end of his first full season with the 76ers Chamberlain found himself battling the Celtics again in the Eastern finals. Wilt had high hopes for the long-sought championship when Philadelphia pushed Boston into the seventh game of the series. But he experienced still another disappointing loss.

In the 1965-66 season, however, Wilt and the 76ers appeared to be close to their goal. On the final day of the season they nosed out Boston for first place. Wilt was voted the Most Valuable Player in the league. The Boston dynasty seemed to be at an end.

Then came the play-offs—and humiliation for Chamberlain. Once more Boston controlled game after game and Russell earned the headlines. And once more the Celtics won—this time, four games to one.

The implication seemed to be clear: no matter how many points he scored, no matter how many records he set, Chamberlain was not a winner. To most people, Wilt represented individual brilliance, but Russell was the symbol of true teamwork—a star on defense and an unselfish feeder whose great

rebounding ignited Boston's fast break. It was even charged that Wilt played for "losers" because his style did not lend itself to team success. His fallaway jump shot—so important in his 100-point game —was a great offensive weapon. But it left him out of position for the rebound. His abundant shooting, some believed, discouraged his teammates, who felt they were only extras in a one-man show. His sometimes less than tenacious defense kept him from fouling out of games, but it also allowed his opponents to score more points. Most fans and players considered Russell, not Chamberlain, the greatest center in the game.

The following year Philadelphia had a new coach. His name was Alex Hannum, the same man who led the St. Louis Hawks to victory over the Celtics in 1958. Earlier, Hannum had earned Wilt's respect as coach of the San Francisco Warriors. Upon joining the 76ers, he set about to improve Wilt's play. Hannum had other talented players to work with, too: Hal Greer, a great shooter and All-Pro guard; Wally Jones, a slick passer who played tough defense in the backcourt; Luke Jackson, a powerful, 6-foot 9-inch forward; Chet Walker, a smooth, 6-foot 5-inch cornerman; and young Bill Cunningham, one of the best "sixth men" in the league. Hannum convinced Wilt that, with such formidable teammates, he could concentrate less on shooting.

Chamberlain is checked by Russell.

Soon Chamberlain was passing off when the defense converged on him, setting up good shots for Walker, Jones or Greer. And, while they were shooting, he took rebounds. When he did shoot, Chamberlain restricted himself primarily to tap-in's, dippers and dunk shots. On defense he became more involved and aggressive, blocking shots and harass-

Wilt passes off to teammate Bill Cunningham.

ing shooters. His style, in fact, began to resemble that of an offense-minded Russell.

The result was a brilliant season for Wilt and the 76ers. They tore apart the N.B.A., finishing first with an all-time record of 68 wins and only 13 defeats. Wilt averaged a relatively low 24.1 points per game, but he still led the league in rebounding and shooting percentage.

Yet, even though the 76ers finished eight games ahead of Boston, they had not proved themselves, for they had to beat the Celtics in the play-offs. And Wilt knew that Russell would be at his toughest with the championship at stake.

Whenever they had met in the past, Chamberlain had usually held a statistical edge over Russell. Even so, since Chamberlain had come into the league, his teams had lost 70 games to Boston and won only 38. Some people felt that Russell had Wilt "psyched;" that is, he had convinced Chamberlain that Boston was always destined to win. Wilt denied it, but sometimes the frustration within him burst to the surface. For example, late in the season Boston had routed the first-place 76ers, despite Wilt's domination of Russell. After the game Chamberlain had snapped: "Tomorrow morning, all across the country, the headlines will say Russell outplayed Chamberlain again. That's what they'll say."

Now the all-important moment had arrived. Boston had defeated New York in the first round of the play-offs and it was time for the Celtics and 76ers to meet once more in the Eastern division finals. The winner would still have to meet the champions of the West, but this was the real test for each team.

Before the first game in Philadelphia, Wilt appeared relaxed and happy. The hometown fans cheered him mightily when he strode onto the court. If he had doubts, he didn't show them.

Wilt and Russell confronted each other in the midcourt circle before the opening tap. Russell had become Boston's player-coach at the start of the season, and Chamberlain leaned across and grinned as he whispered in Russell's ear: "You've done a nice job of coaching. But I'm going to break that up tonight."

As soon as the ball was put into play, Chamberlain set out to fulfill his promise. Batting down shots, dominating the backboards and scoring from the inside, he led the 76ers to a 32-26 lead. Greer and Jones were hitting, too, and the Celtics seemed to lack their old spirit. The score was 66-49 at half time and the 76ers lengthened their lead to 91-66 midway through the third quarter.

Then the Celtics began one of their famous comebacks. Relentlessly they cut into Philadelphia's lead. John Havlicek and Russell were scoring now

The 76ers' Hal Greer grabs a loose ball during the second game.

and Philadelphia fans were angry and nervous, expecting the worst. But with the margin down to 107-96 and history seeming to repeat itself, Wilt made the big play of the game. As the Celtics came down the court, they passed to John Havlicek at the top of the foul circle, where he is usually deadly. But the shot never reached the basket, for Wilt's huge hand actually grasped the ball in midair as though it was a tiny apple and fired it downcourt in one incredible motion. Greer was alone at the other end of the court and he took the pass and dropped in a lay-up to break the game open. Philadelphia went on to win, 127-113. Wilt had scored 24 points and out-rebounded Russell, 32-15.

Two days later the teams resumed their battle in Boston. This time Russell was stronger on the boards. Havlicek and Bailey Howell were scoring consistently and the boisterous Boston crowd was going wild. As half time approached, the Celtics led, 58-47. Then Chamberlain asserted himself, out-fighting Russell for rebounds and feeding the ball to Walker and Jones. Boston's lead was down to 58-55 at the half. After intermission, Philadelphia continued to chip away at the lead as Jones hit with long, jack-knifing jump shots. Wilt hardly shot at all, but his rebounding dominated the backboards. Early in the fourth quarter Philadelphia went ahead, 89-75.

To counter the 76ers' offense, Russell sent the Celtics into a full-court press, using four guards. As a result, the 76ers began to lose the ball and their lead dwindled. With less than 2 minutes remaining, the Celtics reduced the gap to 103-102. Then Wilt was fouled, giving Philadelphia two free throws that could make the difference between winning and losing.

But the 76ers were worried because Chamberlain was known as the worst foul shooter in the league.

That season he had made only 44 percent of his free throws. Wilt aimed, shot—and missed. Boston fans hooted with glee. The big center took a deep breath and tried again. He had to make this one. Swish! Philadelphia led, 104-102.

The Celtics made four desperation shots, but each was off the mark and Chamberlain and Jackson took the rebounds. As the buzzer sounded, Boston heaved a desperation pass down the court. Chamberlain was standing under the basket and, in a gesture of triumph, he extended his fist and punched the ball high into the air. Philadelphia had won, 107-102. Wilt had shot just 11 times and scored only 15 points, but again he had out-rebounded Russell, 29-24.

In the Philadelphia dressing room young Luke Jackson yelled, "It's all over but the shouting!" Wilt, however, had seen too much of Russell and the Celtics to relax. He seemed almost unwilling to enjoy any victory until the 76ers had the N.B.A. title in their hands. "They'll come back just a little bit tougher," he warned.

The next game was played before the largest crowd in the history of indoor basketball in Philadelphia. And Wilt's fears seemed justified when Boston jumped to an early 24-15 lead. Then Chamberlain took control and at the quarter Boston's lead was down to 26-24. Now the 76ers were grabbing

Wilt's passes from the post and scoring on a high percentage of their shots. In contrast, Boston's shooting had gone cold and Wilt was beating the tired Russell under the boards. By half time Philadelphia had a 59-52 lead.

However, the rest period revived Boston. Slowly they narrowed the 76ers' margin. And with just 3 minutes to play the lead was a slim 102-101. But Wilt was still rebounding brilliantly and suddenly his teammates began to hit. Wally Jones fired in three straight jumpers; Walker scored on a drive; Greer dropped in a series of free throws and even Chamberlain hit two of three from the foul line. Then the buzzer sounded and the 76ers were the victors once more, 115-104. Wilt had put on a magnificent performance with 20 points, nine assists and an amazing 41 rebounds. Philadelphia was just one victory away from eliminating the Celtics.

However, once the teams returned to Boston, the situation was reversed. Although Wilt scored 20 points, he missed 10 of 18 shots, plus 7 of 11 free throws, and was out-rebounded by Russell, 28-22. Boston won, 121-117, and suddenly the 76ers were reminded of their past defeats at the hands of the Celtics.

The anxiety of 76er fans began to grow. Many basketball people thought that the Celtics were quite capable of launching another comeback and that Wilt and the 76ers would collapse.

The fifth game opened with the pressure squarely on Chamberlain. If he played badly and Philadelphia lost again, the vital momentum would pass to the Celtics. And, to Chamberlain's supporters, his poor start seemed to be a bad omen. During the first quarter, Boston controlled the boards and sank 16 of 29 shots to take a 37-26 lead. Russell had outrebounded Wilt, 10-5.

The situation went from bad to worse. Havlicek and Larry Siegfried were scoring from all over the court and Boston kept increasing its margin. The 76ers seemed to be standing around, waiting for something to happen. Soon Boston's lead had grown to 63-48.

Then Wilt began to assert himself, scoring consistently and overpowering Russell for rebounds. Slowly the Celtics' lead dwindled until it was down to 70-65 at half time.

In the third quarter Wally Jones suddenly got hot. The little guard's long jump shots kept falling in. Wilt dominated the boards, intimidated Boston shooters with his blocks and kept feeding the ball to Jones, who hit eight of nine shots. Philadelphia led, 100-95, going in to the final quarter and the crowd sensed victory.

Boston was desperate now. Chamberlain leapt high to grab a rebound and he stuffed it through the

(Left) Chamberlain dominated the boards during the play-offs and Russell was unable to contain him. (Above) Wilt and his teammates celebrate their victory over the Celtics.

hoop with two Boston players actually clinging to his massive shoulders. The exhausted Celtics could no longer contain the giant. Walker fed the ball to Cunningham, who drove past Russell to score. Greer swished in a baseline jump shot. Twice Wilt ripped rebounds from Russell's hands and passed to Greer for easy baskets. Havlicek shot, but Wilt blocked it. Russell shot and Wilt slammed it down. The Boston dynasty was coming to an end.

The 76ers continued their scoring rampage up to the last moment. When the buzzer signaled the end of the game, the scoreboard showed: Philadelphia 140, Boston 116. Wilt had finished with 29 points, 36 rebounds and 13 assists.

"Wilt was dedicated out there," Coach Hannum said above the noise in the victors' dressing room. "No rebound was going to get out of his area. No close shot was going to be unblocked. No one was coming through. He made his mind up."

Chamberlain had finally achieved his victory over Boston. And it was all the more meaningful because Russell had also played a brilliant series. During the five games, the Celtics' player-coach had pulled down 117 rebounds, scored 57 points and was credited with 30 assists. But Chamberlain's playing had been inspired and he wound up with 160 rebounds, 108 points and 50 assists, plus dozens of blocked shots.

In the days that followed, Philadelphia wrapped up the N.B.A. championship by defeating San Francisco in six games. Although Chamberlain starred once more, the series with Boston had been Wilt's true moment of glory. After eight agonizing years he was a winner at last.

INDEX